The Media Addict's Handbook

Restoring the Quality of Life in
the Great Age of Mediation

Jeff Einstein

THE MEDIA ADDICT'S HANDBOOK
Copyright © 2013 by Jeff Einstein
All rights reserved.
No part of this book may be used or reproduced in any manner whatsoever without written permission except in the case of brief quotations embodied
in critical articles and reviews.
ISBN-13: 978-0615888842
ISBN-10: 0615888844

Visit mediaaddictshandbook.com for more information.

For Barbara

Introduction

We live in a time when – like the citizens of Aldous Huxley's *Brave New World* – we are mostly undone not by the things we hate, but by the things we love. We are undone not by the things denied to us, but by our insatiable appetites for more of what we already have in excess.

We live in a critical and pivotal time fraught with peril, a time when an indisputable super-addiction to all things media and all things digital is now the default condition of American life, the rule rather than the exception. It's a time when our addiction to all things media and all things digital – like any other addiction to any other narcotic – steals our time and money and freedom and sits imperiously as moderator and potentate over all of our most important individual and collective debates. We live in what I call the *Great Age of Mediation*.

We are born like crack babies in the Great Age of Mediation, addicted to all things media and all things digital from birth, and we remain addicted from cradle to grave by design. We may be students or professionals, unemployed or none of the above, but make no mistake: in the Great Age of

Introduction

Mediation we are media addicts first and foremost, and we behave – predictably and reliably – like addicts addicted to any other drug. We just don't notice it as much as we notice other less prevalent addictions to other less prevalent drugs, perhaps because everyone around us is a media addict also and behaves the same way we do. In the Great Age of Mediation addiction is the new normal.

More ominously, however, our super-addiction to all things media and all things digital invites and all but guarantees profound social consequences, almost all unintended. The early years of the Great Age of Mediation have already witnessed epidemic levels of stress and lifestyle-related illness, several ruinous market bubbles and crashes, chronic unemployment and economic malaise, the rapid consolidation of immense power in huge institutions both private and public and the inexorable, perhaps irreversible erosion of civil liberties, institutional accountability, public trust and the general quality of life. In the Great Age of Mediation we watch the quality of our lives erode before our eyes and euphemize whatever remains as the new normal.

We are – to quote the late great media ecologist Neal Postman – *Amusing Ourselves to Death,* and there's no turning back the clock, no stuffing the high-tech genie back into a somewhat lower-tech bottle. Pulling the plug and abstinence are fast-track solutions to failure in the Great Age of Mediation. The best we can do is hope and work to moderate our own behaviors and find a better and more livable way to co-exist with our super-addiction to all things media and all things digital before it consumes us entirely. We need to restore the quality of life stolen from us over the past generation, and we need to protect the quality of life for future generations. And we need to begin right now. *The Media Addict's Handbook* is my commitment to the deliberate search for a viable way to moderate our behavior and help restore the quality and promise of American life in the Great Age of Mediation.

Structure

Because the primary functional imperatives of pop culture are to sell the present and obliterate the past, I thought it might be of considerable value to begin our sojourn together with *A Brief History of Digital,* an insider's guide to how our super-addiction to all things media and all things digital emerged and evolved in our lives since the introduction and adoption of the microprocessor in the late 1970s and early 80s. *A Brief History of Digital* describes precisely how we got from there to here, and the contrarian lessons gleaned from it infuse and inform the rest of *The Media Addict's Handbook*, structured in a simple and traditional thesis, antithesis, synthesis format as represented by three major sections: *The Quality of Life Defined, The Quality of Life Threatened* and *The Quality of Life Redeemed* – all leading up to a final chapter, *Simple Rules for a Good Life.* Let's take a quick look at each major section now…

Part I: The Quality of Life Defined

Part I explores and offers a working definition for the quality of life, a subject that has rightfully engaged and inspired the genius and imagination of great minds throughout recorded history. My contribution begins by suggesting quite simply that the quality of life is defined by how and

Introduction

where and with whom we spend our time and invest our faith.

I further suggest in Part I that the mechanics of how and where and with whom we spend our time and invest our faith are governed by the rituals that we build around our relationships with everything and everyone in our lives. Rituals – sacred and profane, meaningful and self-serving – dictate how, where and with whom we spend almost every minute of every day; we constantly unfold and consult them like roadmaps to our own lives.

Part II: The Quality of Life Threatened

Part II explains the mechanics of addiction and explores the extraordinary breadth, depth and urgency of our super-addiction to all things media and all things digital. I explain how it steals our time, money and freedom – like every other addiction, regardless of the narcotic – and how it compromises the quality of our lives in all ways: spiritually, socially, emotionally and physically. I explain how it takes over our lives as moderator of all our internal debates, and how addiction as the default social condition in the Great Age of Mediation degrades the integrity of our institutions and communities and threatens the future of our nation.

Part II also introduces the *Media Log* and *Emotional Impact Ladder*:

- The *Media Log* is an abysmally simple yet extremely challenging exercise designed to expose our own complicity in and capacity for excessive media consumption. Fair warning: you might find the *Media Log* both unsettling and disturbing; many do. Predicated on the essential understanding that we simply can't begin to deal with something that we cannot or will not see, the *Media Log* dusts the fingerprints of our unconscious behavior. It renders the invisible visible, and hopefully will motivate a few of us to examine certain behaviors we might otherwise prefer to ignore.

- The *Emotional Impact Ladder* ranks the emotional impact of our most popular communications tools and illustrates how we are compelled to disengage emotionally as we descend its rungs and increase the volume of electronic communications in the Great Age of Mediation.

Part III: The Quality of Life Redeemed

By definition, the Great Age of Mediation offers little hope and even less time for mainstream addiction recovery platitudes and practices like prevention and abstinence. It's simply far too late to prevent what's already ubiquitous from suddenly showing up; that horse left the barn a long time ago. Additionally, the very notion of abstinence in the Great Age of Mediation – the age of trillion-dollar consumer economies powered by billions of microchips – borders on laughably quaint, especially in the near-total absence of champions to praise and model the only viable long-term alternative: moderation.

Part III introduces a far more effective and time-proven methodology to interrupt and moderate the extreme influences and harmful thinking – what recovering addicts some-

Introduction

times refer to as *stinking thinking* – that conspire in the Great Age of Mediation to steal our time and money and otherwise diminish the quality of our lives and communities. In Part III I'll show you how to slow down, how to let go of the behaviors that don't contribute to the quality of your life and how to embark on a path of deliberate simplification. In short, I'll show you how to improve the quality of your life in the Great Age of Mediation.

Here in Part III you'll find the *Human Centrifuge* and *My Ritual Inventory*:

- The *Human Centrifuge* is a perfectly compelling model for life in 21st-century America, a graphic illustration of how the quality of our lives is compromised by the Great Age of Mediation's two most oppressive characteristics: constant acceleration and massive inertia.

- *My Ritual Inventory* is an elegantly simple yet incredibly powerful tool – a sheer gratitude engine – designed to help you identify, restore and sustain quality in every possible facet of your life, and an antidote to the addiction-driven high-tech toxins that poison our lives and destroy the quality of life in the digital 21st century. *My Ritual Inventory* will show you precisely how to introduce moderation and deliberate simplicity into your life as the tonics for what some recovering addicts call *self-will run riot* in the Great Age of Mediation.

The Media Addict's Handbook

Worth Noting...

The *Media Log, Centrifugal Map* and *My Ritual Inventory* have proven themselves in application with many thousands of individuals over the past generation, dating back to the mid-1990s – when I first started to ponder what would happen to our lives in the transition of immensely powerful digital office productivity tools into consumer products. I urge you to spend time with them. Putting them to work in your life will open new doors for you and improve the quality of your life – unequivocally.

Also gratified to report that the media-as-addiction theory that no one took seriously a mere decade or so ago when I first started writing about it in 2004 is suddenly not only much harder to dismiss, but very much a front-burner topic of discussion and debate these days. The reason is simple: Step outside and all you'll see – no matter where you go – is people tethered to their smartphones and tablets like trained dogs on digital leashes. We find smartphones at work, smartphones at the dinner table, smartphones in our synagogues and churches and mosques, smartphones in our classrooms and smartphones in our bedrooms. By now everyone knows that we have a bona fide dependency problem on our hands, and it's simply no longer possible to dismiss the fact that we have become, as Thoreau warned more than 150 years ago, tools of our tools, and very much complicit in our own addiction.

That said, I know from personal experience that many mainstream addiction recovery advocates will doubtless take offense to what they read herein, in no small measure because my thoughts on addiction are largely heretical and refute many of the sacred-cow myths and half-truths about

Introduction

addiction dating all the way back to the early days of Alcoholics Anonymous. The same myths and half-truths still prevail and dominate today (at least in this country), some eight decades later.

You should know, however, that I didn't set out initially to challenge mainstream addiction theory. In fact, when I first began to explore the relationship between media and addiction, I was a diehard and enthusiastic 12-step acolyte. But the more I studied the relationship between the two, the clearer it became to me that how we perceive our own addictions – including and especially our super-addiction to media – is very much influenced and colored by the internal narratives fashioned in self-defense by the addictions themselves. So I was compelled to re-examine my own intellectual and emotional investments en route, and discovered – to my considerable dismay – that they were mired at least as much in popular culture folklore and myth as they were in fact.

But for every mainstream addiction recovery advocate who objects to my theories, there's at least one media professional or academician who will likewise take umbrage with much of what I say. Like their counterparts in the addiction recovery industry, media professionals and academicians have their own canon of sacred cows and half-truths to defend, and with almost three decades of senior media and marketing industry experience under my belt, I've had plenty of occasion to invoke them all a million times or more.

Still, The Media Addict's Handbook is by no one's definition a media industry exposé or critique, nor is it by any standard an exhaustive treatise on addiction and addiction recovery. I simply want to introduce a sober and non-partisan explanation for how and why the quality of our lives is eroding in the Great Age of Mediation, and to explore what we can do about it.

One of the many reasons why no one is ever likely to confuse me with a scholar of any sort is a stubborn refusal and a deliberate decision made many years ago not to cite statistics (at least not very many) in support of my own arguments – a conscious act of omission and a mildly perverse form of modern heresy that some will likely find refreshing and others will just as likely find downright appalling. "There are three kinds of lies," said Mark Twain: "lies, damned lies, and statistics." In the Great Age of Mediation statistics and metrics less frequently describe what works and more frequently describe what can be sold, for how much and to whom. We tend to use them as a form of modern numerology to support all manner of things both savory and unsavory, a disturbingly common practice that almost always compromises and sacrifices the truth along the way. By contrast, my arguments about both addiction and media – although researched and refined over many years – are forged largely in common sense tempered by three decades of personal and professional experience as both an addict and a recognized digital media pioneer. Common sense, I assert, should start the discussion and prevail in the end.

Some critics will no doubt interpret my lack of statistics as evidence of lazy thinking predicated more on faith than fact. So be it. As a gratefully recovered ex-advertising executive, I'm well prepared and trained to accept faith over fact any day; it pays better and is far more accountable in the

Introduction

end. On a related note, I discovered long ago that only faith gets me out of bed in the morning, and that the facts are typically far too subject to whimsical, partisan, and wholly expedient interpretation by self-anointed experts, patriots and scoundrels alike. These days the facts are wholly unaccountable by design, and with all due respect, today's newspaper headlines are tomorrow's fish wrap.

The lack of statistics notwithstanding, the highly contrarian nature of these pages can be explained in large part by a working philosophy borrowed from what I call the *Albert Keeler Principle,* an amalgam of two sage observations from two great Americans, Albert Einstein and Wee Willy Keeler: Einstein said no problem can be solved by the same thinking that created the problem, and Wee Willy Keeler counseled us to keep a clear eye and hit 'em where they ain't. Add it all together and it's easy to understand why no one ever hired me to promote the status quo. Nevertheless, I think you'll find my arguments about both addiction and media to be not only sensible and well-reasoned, but invigorating and liberating as well. At least I hope so, though I would encourage you nevertheless to research the numbers and facts yourself to corroborate or refute any of my arguments. Knock yourself out if it makes you feel better, and if you find something worth noting, please pass it along.

Please know also that I'm always prepared and eager to defend my assertions. I invite debate in no small part as redemption for my own contributions to the present dilemma, dating all the way back to 1984, when I authored the first major how-to book series on personal computers and co-founded the nation's first digital advertising agency. Since then I've counseled thousands of individuals and dozens of institutions – corporate, civic and religious – on the true functions and effects of media and digital technology on our lives both at work and at home, always with compassion and humor and always with the same objective: how to improve the quality of life in the Great Age of Mediation.

As an early pioneer drunk with ambition in the Great Age of Mediation, I taught people how to make a living *from* digital media and technology. More sober now, I teach people how to live *with* our addictions to the same digital media and technology. *The Media Addict's Handbook* reflects much of what I have learned over the years about my personal relationships with technology and media and my addictions to both, and I offer it now to you as a step-by-step guide to a better, richer, more integrated life as we continue on our individual and collective sojourns through the Great Age of Mediation. I can unconditionally promise and guarantee no shortcuts en route, and would suggest that you hold on to your wallet if and when you encounter someone who promises otherwise. Make no mistake: God moves mountains, but you and I are better advised to bring our own shovels...

Jeff Einstein
June 2013

A Brief History of Digital Whoops...

Popular culture by definition cannot tolerate critical self-examination. It simply cannot pause to turn the spotlight inward, nor can it spare the requisite time to fashion any meaningful historical narrative. Like a shark in the water, popular culture must always keep moving forward or die. Thus is history in the Great Age of Mediation rendered essentially stillborn and inert – at best a quiet and reflective respite from the clamor of the present.

That said, I feel a personal obligation to set the record straight and to provide an explanation for how we suddenly woke up one day to find ourselves so firmly ensconced in the Great Age of Mediation. As is often the case, however, the truth bears little resemblance to popular myth and legend. Though brief, what follows below is wholly unabridged and completely factual...

The 1980s

It may seem hard to believe these days – especially when our personal lives are so crammed with so many digital devices – but the digital revolution didn't begin at home. It didn't begin at home simply because there was no functional or otherwise compelling reason for consumers to buy personal computers in the late 1970s and early 1980s, so the home market fizzled out soon enough and didn't re-emerge in strength until the mid-1990s with the rise of the Internet. Instead, the digital revolution began in the office where applications for PCs were patently obvious, and it came of age not with the introduction of the personal computer as a consumer product in the late 1970s and early 80s, but with the adoption, maturation and utter ubiquity of the electronic spreadsheet as the dominant corporate tool just a few years later. The sudden ability to project and manipulate corporate numbers with a facility and scale previously impossible and unimagined delivered immense power to the captains of industry and finance and gave rise to a high-tech Wall Street culture whose influence and dominance continues to grow virtually unabated in direct relationship to the power and ubiquity of the chips and devices that power it.

"We shape our tools and thereafter our tools shape us."
– Marshall McLuhan

The sudden flurry of M&A activity, the Black Monday stock market crash of October 1987, and the collapse of the savings and loan industry later in the same decade were all early manifestations of an overly enthusiastic corporate rush to adopt and deploy a digital tool whose inherent power and sudden ability to project immense scale far surpassed our limited ability to mitigate and moderate any associated risk.

Meanwhile, the introduction of cable TV in the early 1980s fragmented urban audiences and forever changed the commercial media landscape. In lieu of the ability to reach mass audiences like their established broadcast counterparts, the fledgling cable networks sold the ability to target their audiences much more efficiently instead. Suddenly, agency media planners and buyers were besieged by armies of cable network sales reps, all of whom extolled the virtues of effective targeting based on extensive data-driven audience research. The working vernacular of advertising and marketing began to change accordingly as the primary industry focus, infrastructure and billing mechanisms shifted away from creative execution and moved towards media, a tool-driven migration made possible and powered by the wholesale adoption and application of the electronic spreadsheet. The sheer number-crunching power, appeal and corporate ubiquity of the electronic spreadsheet all but guaranteed the corresponding migration of agency resources from the message to the medium and – true to the sage observation of pioneer media ecologist Marshall McLuhan – the medium indeed became the message.

Still, someone had to sell the surging Wall Street and high-tech cultures (not to mention all the digital hardware and software that rode shotgun with them) to Main Street America. Enter the production-line template for the postmodern MBA, a thoroughly digital technocrat formally trained in both marketing and financial disciplines. It's no mistake that the equally rapid ascents of the Wall Street and digital media cultures coincided, as both were driven by graduates of the same MBA programs of the same schools, and both were favored stepchildren of the exact same tool: the electronic spreadsheet – without a doubt the most powerful, persuasive and thoroughly abused technology of all time.

The 1990s

The explosive evangelism of the World Wide Web as a commercial medium and the financial promiscuity of the brief dot com era that rode shotgun with it were entirely consistent with the characteristics of a media-driven youth movement, not unlike the one that spread rock and roll and free love around the world via commercial radio and TV in the 1960s. During the six years between 1995 and 2000, legions of youthful MBAs – most with little or no actual hands-on experience in marketing and advertising – assumed complete control over what would soon become history's most potent and powerful medium.

Despite the counterculture hype, these were hardly the rogue advertising madmen of yesteryear. And they weren't equipped with mere slogans and taglines. These were highly motivated, highly educated and highly financed young MBAs equipped with the most powerful business tools ever devised, tools powerful enough to eclipse even the hard-driving ambitions of those who deployed them. The young dot com evangelists were the 1990s versions of the highly motivated, highly educated and highly financed young physicists and scientists who gathered in Los Alamos during World War II to build the first atomic bomb. This generation, however, wasn't hired and funded by a wartime government and didn't crunch their numbers with slide rules, chalkboards and mechanical calculators. This generation was hired and funded instead by huge technology companies and rapacious venture capitalists, and their calculations were powered by a billion microchips. And just as the young physicists and scientists of Los Alamos ushered in the Nuclear Age, the young technologists and MBAs of the Silicon Valley in California and the Silicon Alley in New York City ushered in the Great Age of Mediation.

Safe to say that neither generation was particularly inclined to ponder the long-term consequences of their respective efforts and technologies, as youth on a mission rarely are. Hence, the young Turks of the dot com era didn't think twice about what might happen to our lives and our lifestyles as they engineered and fast-tracked the migration of immensely powerful digital office productivity tools – like laptops, PDAs and mobile phones – from the office into our homes. No one pondered what might happen once most of the functional distinctions between the office and the home were obliterated, or what might ensue as the pace of our private lives accelerated to match the speed of our own office technologies. No one paused to consider how the promise of immense digital scale might soon all but eliminate institutional accountability and erode the public trust, nor were there any Surgeon General warnings affixed to any of the digital devices we slipped in and out of our pockets and purses dozens of times each day like packs of cigarettes…

> WARNING: *This device is exceptionally addictive. It was not designed to improve the quality of your life. It was designed specifically and explicitly to increase productivity. Its use will guarantee profound unintended consequences – some of them not so good.*

Of course, no one thought the dot com boom would ever end, either. At least not until it came crashing down in the spring of 1999. But by then the damage was done: commercial media poured unabated through the digital pipeline and flooded absolutely everything. By the end of the dot com era our lives had been vastly accelerated and forever changed – not necessarily for the better.

The 2000s

While high-tech investments in the mid-to-late 1990s focused primarily on building out the essential commercial architecture and infrastructure of the Internet, the first decade of the 21st century was mostly about three things:

1. **The consolidation of power.** The first decade of the 21st century was one of immense mergers and acquisitions among already enormous media franchises, especially online. In addition, huge amounts of investment capital were put to work on commercial technologies that would a) rapidly expand and set the stage for broadband access and b) track, analyze and optimize consumer behavioral data online. Sure enough, broadband access soon became the de facto standard while the digital advertising and marketing industry – in response to legitimate consumer concerns about the volume and integrity of the behavioral data tracked, analyzed and optimized – solemnly promised on a stack of shrink-wrapped user manuals to regulate itself, and embarked on a mission to educate consumers not to worry so much about potential abuses of personal data. Your data, they promised, are safe, and the fact that we track, analyze, parse and sell them to anyone who asks is merely the price you pay for a far better and far more efficient online experience. "Trust us," they said.

   Of course, soon after 9/11 government security and intelligence agencies were granted broad powers by Congress and executive order to deploy the same basic digital tracking technologies in the war against terrorism with the same basic refrain: Your data are safe, and the fact that we track, analyze, parse and share them is the price you pay for a secure homeland. "Trust us," they said. Meanwhile, the government directive to the commercial high-tech and media industries was likewise simple and to the point: "We now have the legal right and legitimate excuse to subpoena and examine your customer data pretty much whenever we want. So let's do lunch and partner up."

Thus we were taught by industry and government agents alike not to worry about all of the digital tracking and spying technologies we couldn't see at work behind the scenes. "Pay no attention" they told us, "to the man behind the curtain."

Meanwhile, those who stood the most to gain by selling digital technologies and media to everyone on the planet evangelized the liberating, lifestyle-enhancing and presumed democratizing effects of their products and services, and proclaimed the entire world on-demand and at our fingertips. True enough, perhaps, but behind the scenes the real byproducts of so much digital power in the hands of so many huge institutions were...

a) corporatist collusion of private and government interests on a massive scale,

b) the equally massive expansion of immensely amplified institutional power along with

c) the rise of unmanageable complexity and the virtual end of institutional accountability.

The medium was the message and the true message of digital media was buried far beneath the graphic user interfaces that whisked us like magic from one virtual reality to another. The medium was the message and the true message of digital media was far less about the democratization of media as advertised and far more about the consolidation, expansion and unaccountability of institutional power.

2. **Online and on-demand video and HDTV.** By 2005 high-speed Internet access was already the rule rather than the exception, and what hadn't yet been obvious to some soon became obvious to everyone: a) that broadband Internet access was in fact all about the distribution and consumption of video on demand, and b) that video on demand – especially HDTV – was by far the most powerful and influential drug in history. No surprise therefore that by the end of the 21st century's first decade, virtually every digital device on the planet came equipped with an HDTV screen, more than half of all Internet bandwidth was devoted to uploading, downloading and streaming on-demand video, and HDTV was the broadcast standard mandated by governments worldwide.

3. **Mobile.** The introduction of the smartphone liberated on-demand video and all but completed our enslavement as media addicts. We now had access to our favorite and most reliable media narcotics 24/7 – sitting, standing or flat on our backs – whenever we wanted, wherever we went.

Of course no brief history of the 21st century's first decade would be complete without mention of the great housing collapse and market crash of 2007 and 2008 – the third and fourth major market crashes to occur in the debut generation of the electronic spreadsheet. Rather than explore our own complicity in the tool-driven nature of each financial debacle, however, we conveniently added three zeros to the national dialog and debt after each crash, crunched the new numbers and partied on – all of which seemed a pretty livable arrangement until late 2008, when we suddenly ran out of zeros because no one knew what to call a thousand trillions...

Part I

The Quality of Life
Defined

Chapter 1
The quality of life as a function of time and faith...

Although we may find it difficult to agree on what exactly constitutes quality, we typically know it when we encounter it. Most quality things simply stand out from their less quality counterparts. They seem to command and reveal more reverence for and attention to detail, even a greater appreciation for the very time and space they occupy. Quality often surprises us, perhaps because it's one of those things that frequently finds us when we open ourselves to it in serendipitous moments. Yet it doesn't seem to matter what form quality assumes or where or how I encounter it – in a great book, a beautiful song or a fabulous meal with good friends. Every encounter with quality makes me feel good and happy to be alive. All of which leads me to conclude quite simply that quality is a gift, a gift we give to others and a gift others give to us.

While we can certainly aspire to the knowledge of God (at our own considerable risk), we simply cannot

Chapter 1

know with any measure of real certainty what awaits us from moment to moment, so we live our lives – by necessity – less in reason and more in faith, burdened by our own mortality and a glaring lack of viable alternatives. The quality we encounter amidst the uncertainty and chaos of our lives imposes meaning and order.

And while we cannot know with certainty what awaits us just around the next bend, the many good things in our lives – some of which seem to come to us in spite of ourselves – confirm that we're not the only ones working on our own behalf. Quality is reciprocal. In the end our appreciation for all of the good things in our lives is measured in the amount of time and attention that we actually lavish on them.

Time of course is our most precious inventory. Time on this earth – however long or short – is the first and most valuable gift given to us at birth. Of all the precious gifts bestowed upon us, however, time is the only one we cannot replenish, the only one we cannot replace. We can replenish our faith, replenish our health, replenish our money, and sometimes even redeem and replenish abused trust. But once our time is gone, it's gone forever, never to return.

Time is our most precious inventory.

Time in the Great Age of Mediation, however, seems to be in pretty short supply. Chronic time starvation is the most frequent and ubiquitous complaint of modern life; it's the default condition from which rises the 21st century's most common and predictable refrain: "If only I had more time."

We are forever complaining about the dearth of time in our lives: Not enough time to spend with my spouse. Not enough time to spend with my kids. Not enough time to spend with my friends. Not enough time to spend with my hobbies. Not enough down time, not enough up time, not enough quality time. The litany of things we simply don't have time for anymore seems to stretch on forever.

Ironically, we are so consumed by our own perception of chronic time deprivation that we devote hours each week to prioritizing our schedules, when we would probably be much better advised to take just a few minutes each day to re-examine and schedule our priorities instead – per the pithy title of lifestyle guru Stephen Covey's book, *First Things First.* Our lives in the Great Age of Mediation will become more livable only when we learn how to schedule our priorities before we try to manage our time.

We need to schedule our priorities before we prioritize our schedules.

Yet how is it even remotely possible to exhaust our most precious resource in the Great Age of Mediation? How can we run out of time when we are so utterly immersed in and consumed with so much time-saving technology? I once added up all of the time I've spent in the past 25 years just rebooting my PC in the office and at home. I predicated my calculations on a conservative (for me) estimate of two reboots every weekday, at three minutes per reboot...

$$\begin{aligned} &2 \text{ reboots} \times 3 \text{ minutes/reboot} \times 5 \text{ days/week} \\ &= 30 \text{ minutes/week} \\ &\times 50 \text{ weeks (two weeks off)} \\ &= 1,500 \text{ min/year} \\ &= 25 \text{ hours/year} \\ &\times 30 \text{ years} \\ &= 750 \text{ hours} \\ &= 31 \text{ days} \end{aligned}$$

An entire month of my life dedicated exclusively to watching my computer reboot – gone forever. The Great Age of Mediation is full of ironies and contradictions, not least among them that we are now compelled to commit so much of our time to the care and feeding of our time-saving devices. Each new device or new app we add to our lives demands a measure of our time and attention – and steals it from something or someone else. Thus the excess that in part defines the Great Age of Mediation almost always sneaks up on us, bit by bit. And every bit of it takes time, the one thing we can't manufacture more of.

We behave, however, as if chronic time starvation is somehow ordained by a Higher Power. But it's not, not in this or any other era. The universe determines only the dates that we enter and exit this life. Exactly how we choose to spend the time between those dates, however, is largely up to us.

Nevertheless, we predicate our behavior on our perceptions, not on our realities, and we perceive ourselves as chronically time-starved, so we behave accordingly. But how does the perception of chronic time deprivation change our behavior? How do we assess the loss of time in our lives, how do we respond to the loss, and what do we sacrifice in the process?

I suggest that what we most fear losing, what we feel slipping inexorably away from us in the Great Age of Mediation, is the very quality of our lives, no matter how we define it. We fear losing our families, we fear losing our homes, we fear losing our jobs and incomes, we fear losing our freedoms, we fear losing our reputations, and we even fear losing our minds. We fear the loss of quality things in our lives because we've already sacrificed what's most important to us – our faith – to the false gods of reason and technology. So we compensate with quantity instead.

Thus the perception of deprivation drives the reality of excess.

A Native American shaman once explained to me his theory for why European Americans are so enthralled with houseplants. "It's because you fear the loss," he told me. "It's because of the distance you place between yourself and your own god. When the autumn leaves turn brown and fall from the trees in preparation for winter, you no longer believe in your heart of hearts that the Great Spirit will return and renew the green in the springtime. Instead, you gather all of the potted green you can and bring it into your home. You horde the green so you won't feel the loss." The real loss in the

Chapter 1

shaman's allegory of course had nothing to do with houseplants. He was talking about the loss of faith and the corresponding replacement of quality with quantity.

En route from deprivation to excess, however, our fear of loss prevents us from taking the time to appreciate and attend to the good things in life. We're much too busy it seems just circling the wagons. But we cannot hope to recognize the quality in something that we simply won't take the time to appreciate. The more fearful we become, the less inclined we are to create time in our already impossible schedules to appreciate and attend to all of the wonderful people and things in our lives. And the less time we take to appreciate and attend to all of the wonderful people and things in our lives, the easier it becomes to neglect or dismiss them the next time we run short on time. The more practiced and efficient we become at neglect for the good people and things around us, the harder it becomes to have faith in anything or anyone other than ourselves, and the harder it becomes to have faith in anything or anyone other than ourselves, the harder it becomes to appreciate the hand of fate at work in our lives. Appreciation therefore is a conscious act of commission; it always precedes the recognition of quality as an act of faith, and it requires practice. Appreciation – like excess – takes time.

Unfortunately, it's difficult to sustain an environment that will support both appreciation and excess. We simply don't have the time to entertain both. Consequently, we begin to lose our ability to recognize quality in others the very moment we stop investing the time to look for and appreciate it in our own lives, the very moment we begin to value quantity over quality. Again, we simply cannot expect to recognize quality in what we do not take the time to appreciate. Orphaned in the mad rush and cacophony of our technocratic lifestyles in the Great Age of Mediation, the quality of our lives withers from sheer neglect.

While we may not be able to dictate exactly when we are born or precisely how and when we die, we can most certainly influence how we spend the time given to us between those two moments. Among the many gifts bestowed upon us – for better or worse – is free will. Even the most diehard addict chooses the daily behaviors that raise the prison bars of his addiction. Yet the same diehard addict can choose behaviors that will lower those same bars. Such small miracles occur millions of times each and every day.

The primary difference between an addict and a recovering or recovered addict, like the difference between bear and bull markets, is faith.

Likewise, the active presence of quality in our lives is a conscious act of faith, an act of choice, an act of free will.

On further examination, therefore, we begin to notice that the quality of life is an essential function of time and faith. More specifically, we begin to see that...

the quality of life is a reflection of how and where and with whom we invest our time and faith.

Chapter 2
Ritual: Arbiter of time and faith...

If the quality of our lives largely reflects how and where and with whom we choose to spend our time and invest our faith, then it makes sense to examine the actual mechanics of how and where and with whom we choose to spend and invest them. How do we parcel our time and faith, and what structures do we erect around them to guide and arbitrate the choices we make about how and where and with whom we choose to spend and invest them? How do the mechanics of how and where and with whom we choose to spend our time and invest our faith in the Great Age of Mediation actually work?

While we may prefer to think of ourselves as rational actors on a rational stage in an enlightened post-modern world, the actual mechanics of how, where and with whom we spend our time and invest our faith haven't changed very much since the early days of tribal civilization.

Chapter 2

We've always invested our time and faith pretty much the same way: in pursuit of the many and varied relationships – rational and irrational – that in aggregate constitute the fabrics of our lives.

We have relationships with our gods, relationships with family, relationships with other people, relationships with authority, relationships with the earth and the other species that populate it, relationships with community, relationships with work, relationships with money, relationships with food, relationships with our bodies, relationships with institutions, relationships with art, relationships with our passions, relationships with our toys, relationships with our creditors, relationships with our technologies, and relationships with our obsessions and addictions. Life in the Great Age of Mediation is an increasingly complex tapestry of interwoven and largely mediated relationships, each of which – for better or worse – demands a measure of our time and attention.

Whatever value our relationships accrue in our lives is assigned to them when we decide how much time and attention they require or deserve.

We simply devote more time and attention to relationships with those things and people that we deem more important to us for whatever reason. We enter into some relationships by choice; others are sometimes thrust upon us by a confluence of circumstance, external mandate or even the inevitable riptide of protracted neglect.

The amount of time and attention we devote to the relationships in our lives may change with circumstance, but our investments in time and attention always reveal current snapshots of our deepest values en route. Our investments in time and attention always expose the hierarchy of our priorities to the bone. What was important to us yesterday may be less so today, and today's afterthought may be tomorrow's headline, but you can pretty much rest assured:

Your current values are a reflection of how and where you currently invest your time and faith, and vice versa: how and where you currently invest your time and faith will reflect your values.

Once the decision is made to invest our time and faith in a specific relationship, the mechanics of those investments are governed by the rituals we build to service it.

How and where and with whom we spend our time and invest our faith is governed by the rituals we build to service each of our many relationships.

Simply defined, rituals are routinely scheduled activities that we erect to service and facilitate our relationships with other people and things; they govern exactly how we invest our time and faith. We devise and deploy rituals to cover each and every relationship in and virtually every minute of our lives. Rituals govern what we do when we wake up in the morning, how we get to work, what we do and how we perform at work, how and when we get home, what we do when we get there, and how we retire for the night. Clearly, our rituals determine how and where and with whom we choose to spend our time and invest our faith.

But not all rituals impart the same value or function the same way.

As arbiters of quality, the rituals in our lives can be classified as either self-serving or meaningful.

Self-serving rituals are those we devise and erect in fealty to our obsessions and addictions. They reflect only our own narcissism, fears and cravings, and cannot by definition be invoked to help ourselves or anyone else. Self-serving rituals are essentially toxic; they typically value quantity over quality, promote excess over moderation, convenience over ethics, and the perception of deprivation over abundance. Reactive by nature, they insert distance between us and our spiritual selves. By contrast, meaningful rituals are those we devise and erect to enhance and promote our own spiritual, social, emotional and physical wellbeing, and the spiritual, social, emotional, and physical wellbeing of others. Meaningful rituals typically value quality over quantity, promote moderation over excess, ethics over convenience, and abundance over the perception of deprivation. Proactive by nature, they draw us closer to our spiritual selves. Meaningful rituals build while their self-serving counterparts destroy.

The table below lists and compares the respective attributes of both self-serving and meaningful ritual:

Self-Serving	Meaningful
• promote obsession • promote quantity • promote convenience • are reactive • promote deprivation • distance us from our spiritual selves	• promote moderation • promote quality • promote ethics • are proactive • promote abundance • draw us closer to our spiritual selves

Many recovery experts describe addiction as *ritualized obsessive-compulsive behavior.* As such, self-serving ritual actually promotes and facilitates our addictions. In fact, every one of our addictions – from cigarettes to gambling – is immersed in and defined by self-serving ritual. But if self-serving ritual facilitates and promotes our obsessions and addictions, what practical functions does meaningful ritual provide for us? I'm glad you asked; let's make a list...

Meaningful ritual brings structure to our lives.

In the act of structuring our time and attention, ritual imposes structure on our lives as well. The importance of ritualized structure in our lives is reflected everywhere throughout history, in every society and every culture.

Simply stated, structure is where the rubber hits the road in our lives. Anyone who suddenly loses a job will tell you just how difficult and daunting it is to restructure their time from scratch each and every morning. In fact, anyone who even lives with someone who loses a job will testify to the massive disruption imposed by the sudden loss of structure. It's one of the major reasons why we feel so awkward on the first day or two of every vacation; we suddenly find ourselves away from our familiar support structures and all of the comforting accoutrements that ride shotgun with them. It's why the greatest perceived enemy of Western civilization is anarchy.

Meaningful ritual brings context and continuity to our lives.

Meaningful ritual is much more than just a convenient way to structure our time and attention. Meaningful ritual is how we structure and ascribe value and meaning to the mundane and commonplace things and events in our lives; each ritualized structure we erect comes replete with its own unique suite of colors and textures and tastes and sounds and emotions. Granted, brushing your teeth every morning likely won't win you any awards, but it's an integral part of the same morning ritual that includes waking up on time, dressing, breakfast, getting the kids off to school, and making your way to work – all essential components to the quality of your life. All meaningful ritual provides structure, and structure sculpts the topography, the hills and valleys, the contexts of our lives. Beyond context, however, looms the very real need for continuity. As irrational creatures of faith first and foremost we need to know in our heart of hearts that the sun will rise in the morning and set in the evening; we need to know that the green will return in the spring. Despite our sometimes frantic efforts to escape our pasts, we need the attachment to what was in order to bring meaning and perspective to what is and what will be.

Meaningful ritual makes us conscious of the continuum we inhabit.

Meaningful ritual provides social and spiritual infrastructure in our lives.

All of our social and religious institutions are full of meaningful ritual. It informs our behavior in every courtroom, in every classroom, in every corporate boardroom, and in every single church, synagogue, and mosque on the planet. It guides our interactions with others and with our gods, and tells us what we can reasonably expect from them in return. Meaningful ritual helps us safely reach outside ourselves in a spirit of generosity and compassion; it's well-documented and no accident that local churches and religious institutions are typically far more effective at providing immediate emergency relief and community services than their better-funded government and secular NGO counterparts. Meaningful ritual is how we carve out and sustain a place for spirituality in our lives.

Meaningful ritual makes us more conscious and less self-conscious.

Meaningful ritual is detail-intensive; it slows us down and compels us to pay attention to the little things in life. Doing so simply makes us more conscious of the world around us, and less self-conscious, less self-absorbed – probably not a bad thing in a society otherwise benumbed by endemic narcissistic narcosis, an endless fascination with our own reflections. Moreover, as you'll learn later, a good deal of the meaningful ritual in our lives is socially attuned, and relies explicitly on our abilities to cultivate and sustain relationships with other individuals and institutions. Through them we learn not only how the behaviors of others affect our lives, but how our behavior affects the lives of others as well.

Meaningful ritual makes us accountable.

There can be no accountability at any time unless and until we are first and foremost accountable to a power beyond ourselves. Faith in God is emblazoned on our money and carved into our courtrooms and institutions for a reason: not only as a reflection of our spiritual faith, but because we are wired to require and seek an ultimate authority in our lives, sacred or profane. Otherwise, there is no ultimate truth, and all arguments – from saints and sinners alike – are equally valid. And where there is no truth, wherever all truth is rendered relative by man, there can be no real accountability to anyone.

Meaningful ritual reminds us that there is indeed an ultimate authority, a power far greater than ourselves, and a truth that lies far above and beyond any we might fashion for ourselves. Meaningful ritual holds us accountable.

Without meaningful ritual in our lives we would be utterly lost and forsaken. Their absence would paralyze us in a heartbeat. Also important to the overall quality of our lives, therefore, is the ratio of self-serving versus meaningful ritual. In general:

The more we fill our lives with self-serving rituals of our addictions, the less quality of life we will enjoy, whereas more meaningful ritual will generally result in better overall quality of life.

The same ratio of self-serving to meaningful ritual also determines our relative distance from spirituality at any given point in time. The more we occupy our time with self-serving ritual, the more we distance our corporeal selves from our spiritual selves. Conversely, the more we occupy our time with meaningful ritual, the closer we draw our corporeal and spiritual selves together. If there is distance between us and our spirituality, it's only because we put it there.

Finally, therefore, we can conclude that the quality of our lives in the Great Age of Mediation reflects the ratio of self-serving versus meaningful ritual in our lives, and – ultimately – the amount of distance that we place between our corporeal selves and our spiritual selves. In other words:

The quality of our life is a reflection of how and where and with whom we invest our time and faith.

Part II

The Quality of Life
Threatened

Part II

The Quality of Life Thorthread

Chapter 3
Eat all you want, we'll make more...

"The paradox of our time in history is that we have taller buildings but shorter tempers, wider freeways, but narrower viewpoints. We spend more, but have less, we buy more, but enjoy less. We have bigger houses and smaller families, more conveniences, but less time. We have more degrees but less sense, more knowledge, but less judgment, more experts, yet more problems, more medicine, but less wellness.

"We drink too much, smoke too much, spend too recklessly, laugh too little, drive too fast, get too angry, stay up too late, get up too tired, read too little, watch TV too much, and pray too seldom. We have multiplied our possessions, but reduced our values. We talk too much, love too seldom, and hate too often.

"We've learned how to make a living, but not a life. We've added years to life not life to years. We've been all the way to the moon and back, but have trouble crossing the street to meet a new neighbor. We conquered outer

Chapter 3

space but not inner space. We've done larger things, but not better things.

"We've cleaned up the air, but polluted the soul. We've conquered the atom, but not our prejudice. We write more, but learn less. We plan more, but accomplish less. We've learned to rush, but not to wait. We build more computers to hold more information, to produce more copies than ever, but we communicate less and less.

"These are the times of fast foods and slow digestion, big men and small character, steep profits and shallow relationships. These are the days of two incomes but more divorce, fancier houses, but broken homes. These are days of quick trips, disposable diapers, throwaway morality, one night stands, overweight bodies, and pills that do everything from cheer, to quiet, to kill. It is a time when there is much in the showroom window and nothing in the stockroom. A time when technology can bring this letter to you, and a time when you can choose either to share this insight, or to just hit delete..."
- George Carlin

We live in extraordinary times. A mere generation ago, addiction was the exception. But no longer:

In recent years – concurrent with the massive explosion of digital bandwidth in the mid-1990s – obsessive-compulsive behavior and addiction have become the undisputed rule.

Obsessive-compulsive behavior and addiction now represent nothing less than business as usual in the Great Age of Mediation, the new normal. Witness millions of alcoholics, millions of sex addicts, tens of millions of food addicts, tens of millions of nicotine addicts, millions of licit and illicit drug addicts, and millions upon millions more compulsive gamblers, workaholics, and shopaholics. Witness addicts in the bedroom, addicts in the classroom, addicts in the boardroom, addicts in the courtroom and addicts in the locker room. It seems as if we can't throw a brick in the Great Age of Mediation and not hit an addict.

I know it sounds outrageous, and I certainly don't mean to offend anyone, but think about it: How many of us can claim a life devoid of obsessive-compulsive behavior or addiction? Who do you know whose life hasn't been touched directly or indirectly by at least one of the above behaviors or addictions at one time or another? And given the already extensive and ever-expanding litany of recognized addictions in American society, it seems perfectly obvious that we can and often do become addicted to just about any experience or substance that offers us the promise of reliable pleasure and relief over and over again.

Indeed, the more you look around, the less outrageous my default addiction theory sounds. The truth is that almost all of us have engaged in various compulsive behaviors or addictions at various times in our lives (and as you'll see in the very next chapter, the vast majority of us still do). In fact:

Our brains and bodies are very much wired for pleasure and escape, and – consequently – very much wired for addiction.

Chapter 3

Of course some compulsive behaviors and addictions are simply more debilitating and disruptive than others, and most don't travel solo; as one might expect, most obsessive-compulsive behaviors and addictions accompany other compulsive behaviors and addictions. Anyone who has ever attended an AA meeting will testify to the rampant presence of cigarettes and coffee, just as anyone who has ever entered a casino will testify to clouds of cigarette smoke and squadrons of cocktail waitresses.

Search the Internet and you'll find a long litany of medical, pharmacological, and psychological definitions for addiction (mostly from organizations with patently self-serving agendas). Almost every definition of addiction you find, however, is a variation on one of two basic themes:

1. By far the more dominant definition of addiction (at least in this country) – the one adopted by most American healthcare professionals, the criminal justice system and rehab programs (including all 12-step programs) – describes it as an incurable, chronic, progressive and ultimately fatal disease that requires nothing less than immediate medical and/or peer intervention.

2. A small but quite vocal minority, however, defines addiction as a common, normal and largely self-correcting lifestyle coping mechanism that sometimes goes awry. Addiction, they argue, comes and goes and becomes more or less extreme in our lives depending in large part on environmental circumstance.

Basically, the addiction-as-disease advocates argue that addicts are victims of their addictions and victimized in spite of their values, while those who view addiction as a normal lifestyle coping mechanism argue that addicts are not victims at all (at least not of their addictions) and are complicit in their addictions because of their values. Typically, those who advocate the addiction-as-disease model embrace abstinence while those who consider addiction a normal lifestyle coping mechanism dismiss abstinence as naïve and unrealistic. Those who consider addiction a normal lifestyle coping mechanism champion moderation over abstinence.

My personal experience with and observations of addiction over the past few decades have led me to a few conclusions:

- First, that addiction is a normal lifestyle coping mechanism, not a disease. As far as I can tell, not one of the many spurious claims made by addiction-as-disease proponents can withstand serious scrutiny: Addiction is not incurable, it's not necessarily progressive and it rarely threatens our lives.

- That addiction is never about the specific narcotic. Rather, addiction is about addicted behavior, and addicted behavior is pretty much the same regardless of the drug.

- That addiction seems to travel laterally in our lives in a continuum, depending largely on circumstance and environment. We are sometimes not addicted, sometimes more addicted and sometimes less addicted.

- That addiction tends to ride shotgun with and support other obsessive-compulsive behaviors and addictions as a reflection of our environments and values.

- That, contrary to the addition-as-disease model vision of addicts as down-and-out derelicts, most addicts are perfectly functional, with jobs and families and mortgages and – hopefully – plenty to smile about.

- That statistically the vast majority of addicts grow out of or learn to moderate their own addicted behaviors without the benefit of any professional intervention whatsoever.

- And finally, that the root cause of addiction is less physical, less pharmacological, less emotional, and more spiritual. That we turn to addiction as compensation for our spiritual emptiness, for the loss of faith mentioned in the shaman's story earlier. That we turn increasingly towards addiction as we turn increasingly – in the Great Age of Mediation – away from our spirituality. Addiction is a flight from spirituality, a flight and respite from personal accountability and responsibility. It severs our spiritual connection with the rest of the universe, isolates us and turns us inward unto ourselves.

So where's the problem? If addiction is none of the dire things that proponents of the addiction-as-disease model warn us against, what's the beef and why should we care? Here's why…

All addictions – at least, according to Carl Jung – are bad for us, regardless of the narcotic.

All addictions – again, regardless of the narcotic – steal our time, money, freedom and quality of life.

All addictions divert our resources and promote false narratives.

All addictions leave us spiritually impoverished.

All addictions incur unintended consequences, and all addictions invert our consciousness: they compel us to ignore the behaviors that help us and promote the behaviors that hurt us.

In short, time and money and resources devoted to our obsessions and addictions are time and money and resources diverted away from the quality of life.

Chapter 4
If it looks like a duck...

For all of the passion that the topic of addiction understandably invokes in us, we shouldn't fool ourselves: We can argue the definition of addiction ad nauseum, but in the end it doesn't matter much which one we adopt, because in the end:

What makes us addicts has less to do practically with how we define addiction and more to do with how we diagnose and deal with it.

While our respective definitions of addiction may vary, the diagnosis of addiction remains a model of consistency. We almost always predicate our diagnosis of addiction on the exact same criteria, on the exact same elemental observations:

The amount of time and money an addict invests in the procurement and consumption of his or her favorite drug(s).

Chapter 4

The drug itself, however, is incidental; it can be anything: heroin or sex, cocaine or gambling, cigarettes or easy credit, uppers or downers, or any combination of the above. It can be just about anything because contrary to the popular misconception:

Addiction is never about the specific drug. Rather, it's about behavior. It's about how and where we spend our time and money in excess.

If, however, the diagnosis of addiction is predicated on the amount of time and money we invest in our favorite drug(s), what constitutes too much? Where do we draw the line that distinguishes an obsession from addiction? How much time is too much time? How much money is too much money? After all, what may look like a lot of money to you or me may be pocket change to someone else. And some folks undoubtedly have more discretionary time than others. True, we may and typically do draw the lines in different places, but I rather think that addiction is like pornography: We usually know it when we see it (especially when we see it in someone else), which may explain why it's far more likely for your spouse or boss or sibling or friend to diagnose you as a compulsive gambler, sex addict, or alcoholic than your doctor. Indeed, addiction is almost always a lay diagnosis, at least initially. After all, your doctor probably doesn't know very much about how you spend your time or where you spend your money. And if your spouse doesn't already know, it's probably only a matter of time before he or she finds out. In other words: If it looks like a duck...

Now consider: According to the 2004 *Middletown Media Studies*, the first large-scale observational study of American media consumption:

> *The average American adult consumes 11.7 hours of media each and every day. That's 4,270 hours per year of media consumption, almost half a year of media consumption for each and every year of our adult lives, and a full 75% of all our waking time.*

Subsequent *Middletown Media Studies* have confirmed the first. Indeed, our media consumption has only increased over the years with the introduction of smartphone and tablet technologies, across all age groups and virtually all demographics.

Not long after reading the *Middletown Media Studies* report in the spring of 2004 I went to a senior editor at *MediaPost,* a major media industry trade publisher, with an idea for a weekly column about how our addictions to all things media and all things digital compromise our ability to conduct business – pretty much the exact opposite view of every other media industry writer and critic at the time, and still pretty much the exact opposite view of every other media industry writer and critic to this day.

The ironic and contrarian qualities of my media-as-addiction theory were hardly lost on the gentleman seated across from me, and he was intrigued but a little baffled at first. "With your background as a writer and digital pioneer you could have gone anywhere with this idea," he said. "Why did you come to *MediaPost?*"

Chapter 4

"Because," I replied, "everyone in your audience is a media professional who eats, sleeps and breathes media, and just about everyone in media these days eats, sleeps and breathes digital as well. I want to speak to your audience," I told him, "because your audience is comprised of the biggest addicts."

To his credit he didn't summarily eject me from his office. Instead, he empanelled a survey the following week among his media-professional readers to test my media-as-addiction theory. Sure enough, the survey results confirmed my suspicions, common sense prevailed and *Einstein's Corner* was launched.

Remember also that the launch of *Einstein's Corner* was way back in 2004, well before the introduction and utter ubiquity of smartphones or tablets, so there's no doubt that we crossed the line that separates our obsession with media from an addiction to media some time ago, and that we haven't bothered to look back since. If anything, we've stepped on the gas, and our media consumption habits have only accelerated accordingly.

What's almost as astonishing as the amount of media we consume is the very idea that we somehow accept or view it as reasonable (or at least as not unreasonable). But if that's the case, how much is too much? If almost twelve hours of media consumption each and every day was reasonable way back in 2004, how much is unreasonable today – when we walk around with HDTV screens in our hands, pockets and purses everywhere we go?

As with most things, the more media we consume, the more we pay. Like most other commodities (and narcotics), the price of media usually increases relative to the demand.

For instance, just a single generation ago (when average media consumption was only about a third of what it is today), most Americans still watched broadcast TV for free. Now, however, almost all Americans are wired for cable, and the average cable TV bill has increased by more than 90 percent over the past decade alone. Of course nowadays there simply is no more "free" TV to speak of, and soon there won't be much "free" radio left either. Likewise, our monthly ISP and mobile phone bills – which we now take for granted but just ten years ago didn't exist at all for most of us – have more than doubled as well during the same period.

As a nation we now spend more than a trillion dollars annually on the media devices and media we consume.

In fact, we consume so much media through so many different devices and channels that it's functionally impossible for anyone or any institution to know with any certainty just how much money our collective media habits cost us.

Of course, with any other narcotic we typically only pay for what we consume. Not so with media, however. So intense and so insidious is our media addiction that – so far at least – we are willing to pay most of our monthly cable, phone, and ISP bills with little or no regard for actual usage. Apparently, not only are we willing to pay for the media we consume, but we're also willing to pay for the media we don't consume – presumably so we can guarantee easy access to them when we need our next fix. I submit that the mere act of paying for a drug that we don't consume would likely fail to satisfy anyone's definition of sobriety, regard-

Chapter 4

less of the narcotic and regardless of how they define addiction.

Indeed, if we diagnose addiction at least in part as the measure of excessive time and money we invest in our favorite drug(s), then the diagnosis of what's on the table in front of us in the Great Age of Mediation is as crystal clear as our HDTV screens:

We are addicted – as individuals and as a culture – to commercial media and our digital media devices.

Not convinced? Ask yourself: Can I drink beer for 12 hours each day and not be an alcoholic? Can I smoke cigarette for 12 hours each day every day and not be hooked on nicotine? Can I gamble for 12 hours each day every day and not be a compulsive gambler? Can I watch online porn or frequent adult chat rooms for 12 hours each day every day and not be a sex addict? Can I shop for 12 hours each day every day and not be a shopaholic? Or perhaps you simply don't believe the consumption numbers in the *Middletown Media Studies* report. Go ahead, cut the numbers in half, and then ask yourself the same question. No matter how we slice it:

We invest more time and more money in media consumption than we invest in any other discretionary activity in our lives – including sleep – by far.

Of course no one puts a gun to our heads and forces us to watch TV or surf the Internet against our will. Media addiction, like all other addictions, is purely a demand-side problem, and almost no supply-side interdiction will diminish the demand for more, not with media and not with any other narcotic. Again: If it looks like a duck...

Several thousand years ago the ancient Vedic Seers observed that we become our attention over time.

They observed that we have a tendency to assume the characteristics of those things to which we devote our time and attention. Thus, if we spend more time with God, they reasoned, we become more God-like. As we think in our hearts and minds, so we will become...

Let's turn our attention now to the *Media Log*, a simple experiment designed to determine how much time and attention we devote to the media in our lives. The *Media Log* is based on two simple assertions, namely: that we can't deal with something that we can't see or fail to examine in the first place, and that a good measure of our daily media consumption is unconscious.

The *Media Log* renders the invisible visible and helps us understand exactly how we become our attention. It was designed to raise our awareness, to make us conscious of how and where and with whom we engage the media, particularly electronic media, and thereby how and where and with whom we spend our time and faith.

So take a look at and feel free to copy the form on the next page...

Media Log		
Time	Medium	Foreground/Background

As you can see from the form, the *Media Log* exercise itself is the essence of simplicity: All you do is jot down every encounter with media throughout one typical weekday. Electronic media include the usual suspects: TV, video games, radio, the Internet, email, iPods and other portable music devices and smartphones. Print media include newspapers, magazines, pamphlets, books, and billboards.

For each encounter, record the time of the encounter, the specific medium, and the nature of the encounter: *foreground* or *background*. A foreground encounter is one where you actively engage the medium in the foreground of your consciousness. For instance, listening to the news on the radio, talking on the phone, watching TV, checking your email and reading a book or a billboard all qualify as active engagements with the media, and likewise qualify as foreground encounters.

By contrast, a background encounter is one in which you become aware of the medium but don't directly engage it. Background media are ambient; they blend into the background. You may notice them, but you choose not to actively engage them. Hence, you may notice billboards or graffiti along the highway, but if you don't read them, they qualify only as background encounters. Likewise, you may notice elevator music but not actually listen to it. You may notice the glare of a TV screen in a darkened room, but decide – for whatever reason – not to watch it.

Since the *Media Log* exercise is all about awareness (and not memory), it's better to record each encounter as it occurs – as you become aware of it – rather than rely on your ability to recall it later. Don't be surprised, however, if your worksheet fills up pretty quickly, and don't be surprised if the exercise becomes more and more demanding as the day wears on.

In fact, don't be surprised if you don't make it through an entire day with the *Media Log*. Most people simply don't; I didn't either on my first few attempts. We quit in part because we discover that there are simply too many encounters with media in our lives to record, in part because we frequently encounter or engage multiple media at the same time, and in part because introduction of the *Media Log* exercise itself adds yet another level of engagement and complexity to an already difficult and demanding daily schedule.

Later, when you get the chance, steal a few quiet moments to review the entries in your *Media Log.* You may notice some interesting patterns. For instance, you may notice that the number of background encounters increases disproportionately with the number of recorded entries – likely a result of the suddenly heightened media awareness imposed by the *Media Log* exercise itself; the mere act of observing your own behavior heightens your self-awareness. You may also notice that a large percentage of your total media encounters are aural; they engage you through your ears. (Typically, the media we hear are more emotive – often more irritating or otherwise evocative – than those we just see.) Or you may notice just how frequently you consume print and electronic media at the same time; usually, the print is the foreground encounter, while the electronic media assumes an ambient background role. You may also notice that your foreground encounters with print (including text narrative online) are far more demanding than your foreground encounters with TV and radio, although electronic media in general are far more compelling, evocative and addictive.

Of course the primary revelation that emerges from the *Media Log* exercise by now will come as no surprise to you:

Our lives are totally and irrefutably immersed in media, and we are thoroughly complicit in our own addictions.

Likewise it should come as no surprise that our addiction to the media comes at a price. Every addiction does. All technologies and all addictions – media not least – are Faustian bargains. They all come with a price tag. In the prescient words of media ecologist Neil Postman, penned more than 30 years ago:

> *"The invention of the printing press is an excellent example. Printing fostered the modern idea of individuality but it destroyed the medieval sense of community and social integration. Printing created prose but made poetry into an exotic and elitist form of expression. Printing made modern science possible but transformed religious sensibility into an exercise in superstition. Printing assisted in the growth of the nation-state but, in so doing, made patriotism into a sordid if not a murderous emotion.*
>
> *"Another way of saying this is that a new technology tends to favor some groups of people and harms other groups. School teachers, for example, will, in the long*

run, probably be made obsolete by television, as blacksmiths were made obsolete by the automobile, as balladeers were made obsolete by the printing press. Technological change, in other words, always results in winners and losers."

Yes, all technologies come with hooks attached. There are no free rides, just as no good deeds go unpunished. Although schooled in a yeshiva, a Jewish parochial school, Mr. Postman himself was not a particularly religious man. He was, however, a protégé of the great Catholic prophet and media ecologist Marshall McLuhan, whose brilliant observation that *the medium is the message* rightfully constitutes the cornerstone of all media literacy and media ecology studies worldwide.

But if the medium is indeed the message, what happens to the message when we, dear reader, become addicted to the medium?

What if we wake up one morning to find ourselves suddenly on the painful losing end of our relationship with the media? What if we're already there? Where will we turn for help, and how much will it cost us to fix the problem? What's the price tag, and how do we pay for our addiction to all things media and all thing digital?

One final question to ponder for now: What happens to the quality of our lives when all of our waking time is committed to our addiction?

Chapter 5
And quacks like a duck...

Many who have performed the *Media Log* exercise tell me afterwards that they are simply appalled by their own seemingly endless appetite for all things media. They find themselves dismayed and disappointed by their own suddenly revealed capacity for excess. They feel betrayed, angered and ashamed by their own human weakness and vulnerability, and victimized by their own environments. Nothing unusual or extraordinary whatsoever in those reactions: that's exactly how addicts feel when their addictions are exposed.

In response, some have admitted to pulling the plugs right away on all of their TVs and assorted electronic gadgets. That response, however, misses the point, and – like most New Year's resolutions – usually doesn't remain in effect for very long in any event. True, extreme responses and sudden flights to health sometimes help us feel better initially, but they rarely get us where we want to be in the end, and sometimes do more harm than good.

Admittedly, the *Media Log* was conceived for its shock value. It was designed specifically to disrupt the unconscious patterns of our behavior and jar our sensibilities in the hope that our complicity and capacity for excess would be suddenly and rudely exposed in the process. It works pretty well that way, but the point of the exercise is not to provoke an extreme response. The objective of this book is not to replace one form of extreme behavior with another; many 12-step groups already do that when they seek to replace excess with abstinence. And abstinence is – for the vast majority of addicts – a guarantee of failure. Rather, the ultimate behavioral objective of *The Media Addict's Handbook* is to engender moderation instead. And we have a long ways to go before we can get from here to there. The *Media Log* is but one tiny step in the right direction, just as waking up in the morning is but the overture to a new day. So don't be impatient, because impatience – especially in the Great Age of Mediation – is high on the list of our own worst enemies, and likewise high on the list of things best embodied by a lifestyle immersed in and driven by countless always-on on-demand digital tools.

Only in the Carrollian landscape of the Great Age of Mediation, where up is more often down and down is more often up, is impatience a virtue.

All of the above, however, must be tempered by the sober understanding that we don't start out as addicts in life, just as no one aspires to become one. Addiction, like excess, creeps up on us. We typically ignore its steady encroachment in our lives until something adverse happens, unless or until we somehow bottom out: Maybe a relationship falls apart under the strain. Maybe we lose a job. Maybe our health fails. Or maybe bankruptcy dangles over our heads like the proverbial Sword of Damocles. I speak from personal experience with all of the above. None of it, however, just happened to me. As with everything else in life, my own complicity conspired with circumstance over time. We choose to act out our addictions just as we choose also to ignore the consequences.

Yet how did we arrive at a time when we suddenly know more about the cult of Hollywood than we know about our own family histories? How did we reach the point where we spend more time in front of the TV or with our smartphones and laptops every day than we do with our kids? At what point did our healthcare system become the landfill for all of our media-induced physical and emotional excess? At what point did trillion-dollar market crashes become routine? When did endless entertainment become the focal point of our lives? How and when did such massive excess enter our lives and assume center stage?

For many of us, all of the above just seemed to happen – like the addiction that ensued. It all snuck up on us over the past generation in the Great Age of Mediation. We opened our eyes one day and there we were, suddenly awash in the detritus of our own excess, and bored to tears, in spite of on-demand access to thousands of TV and radio channels, tens of millions of websites, weblogs and podcasts, and hundreds of thousands of downloaded songs and videos – each and every one designed specifically to rivet our attention and keep us occupied, at least for the next few seconds. But again, addiction is cunning that way; it almost always takes us by surprise...

Chapter 5

Can you remember a time in your life – prior to the mid-1990s, prior to the introduction of the Internet and the explosion of digital office productivity tools that sped unimpeded through the digital pipeline from our offices into our homes – when media were not as rapacious or all-consuming in our lives?

Can you remember how much simpler and civil life was before we blurred the once-cardinal distinction between home and office, or before retail stores stayed open seven days a week?

Can you remember family dinners at an actual dinner table? Can you remember what it was like before we bargained away our leisure time for the largely mythic lure of unimagined wealth and early retirement during the heady dot com days? Can you remember a time when children played unmolested and unafraid on the streets and pedophiles didn't seem to threaten them on every street corner? Can you remember a time when you could phone a company and talk to a real human being without wading through endless voice menus, when companies that profess excellent customer service weren't hermetically sealed off from their customers by voicemail and email? Can you remember a time when you knew the bank teller by name and didn't shop for doctors by insurance plan and zip code?

Of course we can't turn back the clock, and the past in reality was rarely if ever as rosy or Utopian as it sometimes seems in retrospect. There's also something to be said for some sort of emotional safe harbor to protect and free us from our own histories. Indeed, modern America was first settled in large part by dissident Protestants who fled their own European histories of religious oppression, and America's history as a nation of immigrants is very much the history of other people who fled other places to escape the tyranny of their own histories.

And while our addiction to media – like all addictions – certainly helps us flee and purge our own histories (and everything else), it offers a false freedom and redemption in exchange. In fact, it doesn't free us at all; again, like all addictions it imprisons us instead. And it doesn't redeem us; it ransoms our freedom for expedience, cheap thrills, and empty promises.

The sudden and massive introduction of digital bandwidth in the mid-1990s imposed immediate and enormous changes on our lives, not least of which was a tsunami of commercial media that rushed in to fill an insatiable digital pipeline – and almost every waking moment of our lives. Not once, however, did we stop to question our own behavior (something not peculiar to Americans, and something we seldom if ever do in any era). Not once did we pause to examine what might happen to us in transition from the analog to the digital age, or how that transition might translate into and affect our lifestyles for better or worse. We were far too busy building digital kingdoms, slaying analog dragons and sipping designer vodkas to notice or care. We were utterly entertained, utterly complicit in, and utterly oblivious to our own excessive behavior.

As mentioned earlier in *A Brief History of Digital*, the sudden explosion of media in the mid-1990s was not just some spontaneous, collective-unconscious youth movement.

Chapter 5

The dot com era that ensued was fueled by hundreds of billions of dollars of investment capital, all of it powered by a billion microchips and hundreds of billions of marketing and advertising dollars. Together, promiscuous money and unbridled technology ushered in The Great Age of Mediation.

We partied for the next five years in what can only be described as a stupefying addictive binge. Then we crashed. And when we awoke the next morning we discovered that our dreams, our money and our time were all long gone – survived only by our digital devices and our addictions to them.

Like most good addicts, however, we started planning for the next party right away. But the dot com promises of endless prosperity and youthful retirement had skipped town, and taken with them many of our dreams and aspirations. In the wake of their speedy exodus they left behind only fear and envy, the true legacies of all addiction.

I remember when I lost my job in 2001, not long after the dot com economy crashed and burned. As a confirmed workaholic who rarely spent fewer than 65 hours per week in the office, it never once occurred to yours truly not to take all of my office productivity tools – my laptop, my PDA, and my cell phone – home with me that final day, despite the fact that I suddenly had no work to do, no meetings to schedule, and no phone calls to make. But I discovered not long afterwards that the presence of so much gratuitous digital technology in my life was kind of like riding a stationary bike: I was going nowhere fast, fully equipped with a speedometer to tell me precisely how fast I wasn't going, and an odometer to tell me exactly how far I hadn't gone. The time I had once filled with work I now filled trying to find or manufacture work. But my digital gadgets, and my obsessions with them, didn't change at all.

As mentioned in Chapter 4, addiction is never about the specific drug. Rather, addiction is about behavior. And the mechanics of addiction are always pretty much the same, irrespective of the drug.

In a nutshell, addiction rewires our brains over time as we ritualize and repeat the same compulsive behaviors again and again. It usurps and co-ops all of our inborn self-protection and self-preservation mechanisms in the process, then puts them to work instead on its own behalf.

That's why it's possible for us as addicts to consistently choose behaviors that we know run contrary to our own better interests, behaviors that we know might result in dire consequences. That's why we insist on that last drink at the bar before we jump in the car to drive home. That's why we place that final bet at the track before running to the bank to cover our losses. That's why we watch that final half hour of late-night television instead of getting some much needed sleep. That's why we insist on surfing the Web or playing a video game on our smartphones by ourselves instead of playing with our kids. We choose to do all of these things despite the fact that we know better.

Chapter 5

Moderating character attributes like common sense, reason, personal ethics, and faith – attributes that ordinarily protect us and promote our welfare – are routinely suppressed, dismissed, and overruled by the more primitive, immediate, and self-destructive demands of our addictions. Those relationships most attuned to excess rise in the hierarchies of our rewired minds while those that champion moderation – including and especially those relationships that feed our spiritual selves – whither in the exchange.

All of our thoughts and aspirations are passed first through the lens of our media addiction, where they are thoroughly assessed and filtered. Those things that promote moderation – like personal values and spiritualty – are filtered out or modified en route. Those things that promote excess in the interest of the addiction are assigned to the fast track.

Thus do our addictions set themselves up as our emotional and intellectual gatekeepers, as the moderators and arbiters of all of our internal debates – the identical functions assumed in recent years by the explosion of commercial media in our lives.

As the primary gatekeeper to and moderator over all of our internal debates, our addiction to media promotes excess and promiscuity in virtually all things, media consumption first and foremost. After all, no one ever got rich by selling less of anything, and contrary to popular belief, the ads aren't there to support the programs; the programs are there to

> *support the ads. Contrary to what our addictions may whisper sweetly in our ears, they're not here to support us; we're here to support them.*

We've all heard ourselves and others claim addiction to specific TV or radio programs. Some folks claim addictions to soap operas, and some are self-professed news junkies. But again, addiction isn't about the specific narcotic. We don't crave the programs just as we don't crave the actual drugs; we crave the feelings – the pleasure and relief – they so reliably invoke. Proof that addiction is not about the specific drug resides in the simple observation that we don't consume less media when our favorite programs get cancelled any more than a heroin addict consumes less heroin when his favorite neighborhood dealer gets pinched. We just find new programs and new dealers to satisfy our habits instead.

> *In the Great Age of Mediation, the media are no longer at our disposal; rather, we are at their disposal.*

For all of the talk about empowered consumers, commercial advertisers target us far more frequently and aggressively than they seek our permission, and greater consumer choice does not necessarily translate into greater freedom. In the Great Age of Mediation we have far more channels but far less diversity of thought. We have more opinions but far less time to consider them. In the end, our super-addiction to all things media and all things digital – like all addictions – resembles a benevolent despot: It provides comfort and succor and false security in exchange for our utter fealty. But even the most benevolent despots are still despots. They don't work for us; we work for them. And even the most benevolent dictators don't always remain so benevolent.

As mentioned earlier, my theories about media as addiction and about addiction as a default condition of 21st-century America have been most severely criticized – not so surprisingly – by people in the media profession, including not only those who produce, buy and sell commercial media, but by those academicians and pedagogues who research media and teach media-related studies in schools and universities as well. For the most part, those engaged in the production and sale of media don't think very highly of those who – ensconced in ivory towers – research and teach media, except when those who produce and sell media are invited to lecture by those who research and teach media. Likewise, those who research and teach media largely distrust and distance themselves from those who – ensconced in corporate board rooms – produce, buy and sell media, except when those who research and teach media are invited to consult by those who produce and sell media.

Of course, neither constituency has much use for yours truly, in part because no one wants to be called an addict, however apropos, and in part because I typically describe those of us who work in or with media as the biggest addicts – just shy of politicians. What both sides share, however, is an abiding willingness to dismiss the power of the media drugs that we collectively produce, buy, sell, research and teach, and an even greater blind faith in the power of our own intellects to somehow inure us against the narcotic effects of the drug that we immerse ourselves in throughout almost every waking hour of every single day. Stated otherwise:

Ours is simply the same old tried-and-true formula for addiction revisited: We dismiss the power of the narcotic while we profess the power to resist it.

There have been many debates in recent years about whether TV and the Internet make us smarter or dumber. But it hardly matters: intellect and reason are historically poor hedges against addiction, and offer even less protection against our addiction to media. In fact, intellect and reason are among addiction's primary tools to enforce its demands and strengthen its grip on us. The smarter we are, the easier it is for us to rationalize our own self-destructive and anti-social behavior. Thus, the media professionals – those of us who produce, buy, sell, research and teach media – may be the (self-professed) smartest rats in the maze, but we're still stuck in the same maze no matter how many times we find the cheese first.

The mere fact that those of us who produce, distribute, buy, sell, and teach media are also the biggest media addicts distinguishes media addiction from all others.

After all, no pharmaceutical company or drug cartel could survive for long if those who produced, distributed, and sold the drugs were addicted to them. Any brewery whose brewers are all alcoholics or any casino whose croupiers are all compulsive gamblers will crumble in a heartbeat. Of all the addictions, only media addiction so reliably imprisons the souls of those who produce, distribute, and sell the narcotic.

Moreover, the mere fact that those of us who produce, distribute, buy, sell, research and teach media are the biggest media addicts is everywhere manifest in the narcotic itself:

The medium is very much the message, and the message is always attuned to sell more media first and foremost – especially when our addiction to all things media and all things digital sits as moderator atop every debate.

Our lives are so crowded with media and digital devices nowadays that there's barely room for anything else at all. One by one, the self-serving rituals we build to sustain and promote our addiction to media replace the more meaningful rituals in our lives and erode the quality of our lives over time. The dinner table eventually gives way to the evening news while the evening news eventually gives way to celebrity worship and idolatry performed in front of individual digital alters in individual rooms and individual pockets. Family picnics in the park on Sunday give way to all-day football coverage replete with all-day eating and drinking binges. The sounds of songbirds in the backyard give way to the sounds of TV in the background. Intimate family discussions give way to a cascade of cryptic instant messages and short texts, communiqués whose real commercial intent – like email and voicemail and social media – is to sequester us, to avoid meaningful communication, defer intimacy, and offer the illusion of accountability.

Let's take a few moments now to examine the true spiritual, physical, emotional and social costs of our super-addiction to all things media and all things digital as individuals and as a society. The following chapters will explore what happens to the quality of our lives when everything in them begins to quack like a duck...

Chapter 6
Spiritual decline in the Great Age of Mediation...

> *We are first and foremost spiritual beings with occasional social, emotional and physical manifestations, and addiction is first and foremost a spiritual problem with occasional social, emotional and physical manifestations.*

Our spirituality brings meaning to the existential aloneness inherent in our physical and material existence. It sees and finds in our existential aloneness an opportunity for personal growth and connection with the universe around us. By contrast, our addictions turn us inward and away from our spiritual and emotional connections with others. En route, the meaningful rituals in our lives are usurped and replaced over time by the self-serving rituals of addiction. The quiet reflection and contemplation required by our spiritual selves to survive intact is buried alive in the cacophonous din that characterizes the Great Age of Mediation. In the Great Age of Mediation we take a deep breath each

Chapter 6

morning but never take the time to exhale throughout the day. We profess faith and spirituality, but practice neither because the practice of spirituality is not about breathing in. The practice of spirituality is about breathing out. Spirituality is in the exhale.

> *"Learn how to exhale, the inhale will take care of itself."*
> -- Carla Melucci Ardito

Time is the only real pre-requisite to all meaningful ritual. Case in point: the real reason for the rapid decline of the newspaper industry over the past decade has less to do with the digital proliferation of other, cheaper news sources or the elevated costs of news gathering, publishing and distribution, and more to do with the disappearance of the lifestyle that once supported the industry. The truth is that no one these days sets aside a few quiet moments in the morning or evening to sit down and read the newspaper. Wondering what happened to the newspaper industry is like clear-cutting all the old-growth forests and wondering what the hell happened to all the spotted owls. Wondering what happened to the quality of our lives is like damning all the rivers and wondering what happened to all the salmon. Good things disappear when we destroy the environments that support them.

Over the years we become less attached to the sacred and more invested in the profane as we divert more and more of our time from the quietude and serenity of the sacred to the self-will run riot of the profane.

We clear cut the spiritual forest and call it progress.

In the process, our super-addiction to all things media and all things digital rightfully interprets any other god or higher power as an existential threat to its own power.

The first function of all addiction is to drive out all competing gods and undermine or sabotage any moderating force that might otherwise challenge its hegemony.

Likewise, the first objective of all addiction is to weaken the moral and ethical fiber of the host in preparation for what will inevitably follow: a perpetual cycle of fear, distrust, envy, and shame, all of which combine not only to protect and promote the interests of the addiction itself, but to threaten the quality of our lives and – not so coincidentally – sell more commercial media as well.

Our addiction to all things media and all things digital is a jealous god, and – like all jealous gods – cannot and will not tolerate the presence of any other gods. And that's where the *Big Lie* enters the picture. Notorious Nazi propaganda chief Joseph Goebbels once observed that when a lie, no matter how outlandish, is repeated often enough it will eventually be accepted as truth. He explained:

> *"If you tell a lie big enough and keep repeating it, people will eventually come to believe it. The lie can be maintained only for such time as the State can shield the people from the political, economic and/or military consequences of the lie. It thus becomes vitally important for the State to use all of its powers to repress dissent, for the*

Chapter 6

truth is the mortal enemy of the lie, and thus by extension, the truth is the greatest enemy of the State."

Perhaps the biggest and most damaging of the big lies repeated ad nauseum by our addiction to all things media and all things digital in the Great Age of Mediation is that organized religion is the sworn enemy of all things socially progressive and forward-thinking.

The truth is otherwise: organized religion is the sworn enemy of our addiction to all things media and all things digital, and the sworn enemy of all other addictions as well. Religion threatens the power of our addictions just as addictions threaten the power of religion. They sell competing gods: one of moderation and the other of excess. What our super-addiction falsely promotes as an epic battle of religious superstition against enlightened reason is in fact our addiction's self-defense mechanism at work – and not very enlightened.

Still, Karl Marx was at least partly right when he declared religion as the opiate of the masses back in the 19th century. But back then there weren't many affordable opiates to choose from in the first place, and that was before the 20th century arrived with the telephone and radio and TV and video games and the Internet and smartphones. The American, French and industrial revolutions of the 18th and 19th centuries had already destroyed Western theocratic power and pronounced God dead. Into the spiritual vacuum rushed technology and godless statism, and together they proved – by any measure – brutally and wholly inadequate.

Freed from the encumbrances of theocratic adventurism, Western religion returned to its roots as heretical change agent and played a largely provocative role in the 20th century as a significant force for freedom and social progress in just about every meaningful social and political movement worldwide – with the notable exception of communism. The true failure of communism was in the puritanical abolition of God and religion in exchange for absolute statism. It finally collapsed from within in 1989 when the Iron Curtain was sucked into the spiritual vacuum of the Soviet Union and its proxies. The Iron Curtain collapsed because there was no spiritual foundation to support it. It collapsed from within, torn down by the spiritually starved East Germans and other Soviet satellites.

Freedom – it seems – is a spiritual yearning.

By the early 21st century few in America needed religion as an opiate anymore, although the main social function of organized religion remained largely heretical: We look now to traditional religion less as an opiate and more appropriately as a quiet and meaningful refuge from the relentless electronic Babel generated by all our other (mostly digital) opiates.

Functionally, organized religions provide us with codes of conduct intended for the most part to curb our more excessive behaviors and anti-social tendencies and protect the quality of individual and community life. Witness the Ten Commandments: they don't tell us what to do as much as they tell us what not to do. By contrast, our addictions tell us precisely what to do; they encourage and promote and celebrate our excessive behaviors and anti-social tendencies. Thus in the addicted madness of the 21st century, organized religion emerges as a force for social moderation, and stands tall as a staunch defender of those much quieter, less convenient but essential things – like family, faith and community – that contribute most to the quality of life and social cohesion. Where science was once heresy in the Renaissance battle of theocratic power versus enlightenment, religion is heresy (once again) in the Great Age of Mediation as the primary institutional hedge in the battle against our super-addiction to all things media and all things digital. Simply stated, traditional religion's primary function in the 21st century is much more aligned with its original calling: to curb excess and protect the quality of life and the integrity of our families and communities by telling us what not to do and helping us set aside the time not to do it.

The biggest of the big lies in the Great Age of Mediation is that we've somehow outgrown religion, and that our super-addiction to all things media and all things digital is a sufficient surrogate.

Yet in the several hundred years since the demise of Western theocratic power, we've somehow discovered plenty of other reasons to suppress plenty of other people and wage plenty of other wars, the most murderous of which have had little or nothing to do with God or any organized religion.

Consider if you will the 20th century, easily the most murderous on record (so far). More than 37 million soldiers and civilians were killed in World War I, and more than 60 million died in World War II. Stalin murdered more than 20 million of his own people. Mao murdered twice that many of his. Pol Pot murdered three million of his countrymen in Cambodia. Religion accounts for none of these deaths. Indeed, these deaths occurred in spiritual vacuums, places where clergy was systematically and methodically purged as prelude to wholesale slaughter. There's a reason why Hitler and Stalin and Mao and Pol Pot all targeted and eradicated their respective clergies right up front: as self-appointed 20th-century demigods themselves, they simply couldn't compete with the moral authority of the real thing, and likewise couldn't tolerate the inevitable comparisons. Now consider the words of Jacob Bronowski, scientist and poet and author of *The Ascent of Man*, as he stands ankle-deep before a camera in the ash ponds of Auschwitz:

> "To this pond were flushed the ashes of some four million people. And that was not done by gas. It was done by arrogance, it was done by dogma, it was done by ignorance. When people believe that they have absolute knowledge, with no test in reality, this is how they behave. This is what men do when they aspire to the knowledge of gods."

Auschwitz and all the other killing fields of the 20th century are what happen when – in our self-congratulatory rush to enlightenment and reason – we replace our search for wisdom and spirituality with a vastly accelerated quest for

Chapter 6

knowledge and the vastly amplified power that rides shotgun with it.

> *I am not going to argue the presence or absence of God here, but I will argue that our super-addiction to all things media and all things digital – like any other addiction – is a religion of a different and more insidious sort, one with an insanely jealous god that simply can't and won't tolerate any fealty or concession to any other god.*

And I will argue further – per Mr. Bronowski's caution – that the technology-driven swap of spirituality and faith for the false knowledge of gods in the Great Age of Mediation is a dangerous fool's errand and an outright bum deal. Consider for a moment these words from an earlier wise man, King Solomon...

> *I said to myself, "I have acquired great wisdom, surpassing all who were over Jerusalem before me; and my mind has had great experience of wisdom and knowledge." And I applied my mind to know wisdom and to know madness and folly. I perceived that this also is but a chasing after wind. For in much wisdom is much vexation, and those who increase knowledge increase sorrow. – Ecclesiastes 1:16-18*

Both Solomon and Bronowski were rational men of faith. They both knew that information is not knowledge and knowledge is not wisdom. They both knew that knowledge is required to interpret information and that wisdom is required to interpret knowledge. They knew that wisdom prevents us from choking to death on our own insufferable conclusions. They knew that wisdom makes the pain of what we know more tolerable and makes humor possible, and that real wisdom is the wisdom to accept the limits of what we can know and what we can do about what we know. Knowledge leads us to the threshold of wisdom, wisdom leads us to the threshold of our spirituality, and our spirituality takes us beyond what we can know. Our spirituality urges us to venture beyond the confines and existential aloneness of our physical and emotional worlds and cross into a much bigger world, an incorporeal but more connected world navigable not by what we know but by blind faith in what we don't know.

Addiction, however, is a flight from faith, a flight from spirituality, and it's much easier for us to flee from something we don't value, just as it was much easier for the Nazis to systematically exterminate the Jews once they were systematically reduced in the media and German culture to vermin. It's simply much easier to avoid the sacred when everything and everyone is rendered profane to begin with.

There can be no profanity when everything and everyone is already profane.

In the Great Age of Mediation, our super-addiction to all things media and all things digital systematically reduces our spirituality to landfill, just another disposable commodity. Our enslavement begins when we adopt the narrative of addiction and dismiss anyone who believes in God or chooses a religious path as a fanatic and backwards-thinking enemy of progress. It's how the Hitlers and Stalins and Maos and Pol Pots of the modern world always begin their reigns of terror.

It bears repeating: the quality of life is a function of how and where and with whom we spend our time and invest our faith. In the Great Age of Mediation, however, we profess spirituality but typically don't make time for it and just as typically don't invest our faith in it. In the Great Age of Mediation we have neither the time nor the faith to feed our souls. But without the moral authority they impose to guide and protect us from ourselves all bets are off and we consign ourselves and our children to a world whose prison yards cannot exceed the size of the HDTV screens in front of us.

Chapter 7
Social decline in the Great Age of Mediation...

Back in the 1950s the family dinner table was our primary source of news, and almost all of it was local. Almost all the news around the dinner table was about our families, our friends and our communities. More important, however, a high percentage of the news discussed around the dinner table was actionable: news of aunt Martha's sick poodle inspired a phone call; news of a distressed neighbor inspired a personal visit with a plate of home-baked cookies; news of a broken stoplight in the town square inspired a petition signed by residents of the town. But all of that changed with the introduction of the network news. Suddenly, the local news around the dinner table was replaced with national and international news delivered by talking suits in New York who neither knew nor cared anything at all about Aunt Martha's sick poodle, the distressed neighbor or the broken stoplight in the town square. Unlike the dinner table news that inspired local action, the network news about national and world events inspired stunned silence and a star-

Chapter 7

struck and thoroughly unearned reverence for the media-driven expertise of media-bred news celebrities with little or no local skin in the game.

Fade out, fade in: six decades later the American dinner table of the 1950s is for much of the country long gone, neglected to death and replaced instead by on-demand TV everywhere and a cynical digital mantra that tells us to think globally and act locally.

These days, almost none of the news that bombards us from every conceivable direction inspires action of any sort, except perhaps to change the channel.

In the Great Age of Mediation our lives and communities mirror the frenetic commercial media landscape that shapes them:

We're more narcissistic and less civil, more fragmented and less cohesive, more polarized and less patient with those who disagree, more fearful and less willing to assume domestic risk, more mired in our own inertia and less inclined to innovate. We insist on more surveillance and regulation to protect us and our communities against our own excessive behaviors and the excessive behaviors of others, and surrender our freedoms in the process.

As our super-addiction to all things media and all things digital consolidates its station as moderator over all our most important debates, we begin to notice that our time and money and freedoms are slipping away from us. As the giant institutions that control our lives become increasingly complex, unmanageable and unaccountable, what's up seems down and what's down seems up, and we withdraw deeper into our addiction. We become increasingly sequestered, anti-social and disillusioned.

No surprise, perhaps, that all of the above observations describe classic symptoms of late-stage addiction. Let's take a look at them now, one at a time…

The Loss of Time, Money & Freedom

All addictions offer a variation on the same simple quid pro quo: our time, money and freedom in exchange for reliable on-demand succor, pleasure and escape. No one I know who still has a job has more free time today than before the Internet flooded our lives with time-saving digital devices in the mid-1990s, and most people I know are working longer hours for less money with less purchasing power, less credit and more debt to show for it. In short, the loss of time and money in the Great Age of Mediation is patently obvious and well-documented. Less obvious, however, is the loss of freedom…

> *"They who can give up essential liberty to obtain a little temporary safety, deserve neither liberty nor safety."*
> – Benjamin Franklin

The loss of freedom is less obvious because we've been taught by our commercial and government overlords in the Great Age of Mediation to confuse freedom of choice with true freedom.

Chapter 7

True freedom, however, is not the freedom to choose but the freedom not to choose, the freedom not to participate. Unfortunately, the freedom not to participate is among the very first casualties of all addiction. All addictions steal from us the essential freedom not to participate, right up front.

Once we surrender the meta-freedom not to participate, it becomes much easier for us over time to exchange other basic rights and freedoms for the same promise of succor, pleasure and escape. Before we know it, our time, our money and our freedoms are gone. Before we know it, we wake up one day to discover that wholesale participation in the Great Age of Mediation is mandatory, not optional. Before we know it, we discover that we can simply no longer not participate. Those who try are marginalized as fanatics or fringe lunatics, and the news media that once stood in a free society as a protective shield against government abuse is suddenly the power structure's primary partner in crime. Meanwhile, our super-addiction to all things media and all things digital drowns us in a virtual tsunami of amusement, diversion and freedom of choice. The loss of real freedom and liberty in the Great Age of Mediation may be more Huxleyan than Orwellian, more *Brave New World* than *1984*, but at the end of the day it doesn't matter much how we lose our freedom, if someone else takes it or if we surrender it willingly: the loss of freedom is still the loss of freedom.

Unmanageable Complexity

Not many of us can claim a life less complex or frenetic today than the one we lived just a short generation ago.

> *One of the many unintended consequences unleashed by our headlong rush to digital in the 1980s, 90s and early 2000s was massive acceleration in the pace and complexity of our personal and institutional lives as immensely powerful digital office productivity tools – re-purposed and re-branded as consumer products – migrated into our homes and personal lives.*

The sheer volume of asynchronous communications that poured through the digital pipeline created a commensurate demand for increasingly complex backend technologies – all of which require periodic updates and optimization. As any systems or software engineer will tell you, however, each new layer of optimization technology produces unintended consequences. System complexity, brittleness and opacity increase with each iteration. Eventually, the system becomes too layered and burdened with optimization technologies and begins to break down. I call the periodic breakdown of over-optimized systems in the Great Age of Mediation *optimized failure.*

> *The trillion-dollar market crashes that punctuated the late 20th and early 21st centuries are perfect examples of optimized failure at work: each successive market crash added corresponding layers of regulation, enforcement mechanisms, expertise and new*

optimization technologies to the mix – all ostensibly designed to fine-tune the system and prevent future market crashes. And all – apparently – to little avail.

Meanwhile, the pace and complexity of life in the Great Age of Mediation continue to increase dramatically as the rules and laws required to govern such massive support systems multiply exponentially. Tens of thousands of new laws are now introduced each year across the country. Each new law requires corresponding deployment, enforcement and reporting mechanisms, and each contributes in turn to the massive inertia that builds over time like a bulwark to protect the status quo from meaningful change.

In such a Kafkaesque environment involuntary non-compliance – the inability not to break the law simply because the law is too complex to know and therefore impossible not to break – becomes the de facto rule rather than the exception.

Examples of systems too big to fail and too complex to succeed without periodic optimized failures of immense scale include the financial markets, the U.S. Tax Code, healthcare, education, the military industrial complex and associated intelligence agencies. None of the aforementioned systems can be fixed by adding more technology or more regulation and all will generate more and more unintended consequences as they continue to grow more and more complex.

Remember, no one intends to become an addict, so almost all consequences of addiction are unintended. Likewise, the vacuum of thought leadership and our utter reliance on the immense complexity of modern systems in the Great Age of Mediation all but guarantee unintended consequences of equally immense magnitude, what author Nicholas Taleb describes as *Black Swans* – major, life-changing social events that catch us entirely by surprise. Black Swan events can be good or bad, natural, supernatural or manmade, but by definition are utterly unpredictable, both in spite and because of our technology.

Optimized failures and Black Swan events are the rules not the exceptions in the Great Age of Mediation.

Likewise, our personal lives become increasingly unmanageable over time with each new layer of institutional complexity. We introduce new technologies and techniques and efficiency experts by the truckload to help us better manage the people, institutions and things in our lives, but each new technology and technique adds additional complexity and ultimately makes our lives even more unmanageable. Eventually, the stress and accelerated demands of life as addicts in the Great Age of Mediation catch up with us and – like the highly complex institutional systems in our lives – we begin to break down. We bottom out: our health fails and/or our finances fail and/or our relationships fail or the institutions around us fail or any combination of the above.

Chapter 7

Contrary to popular addiction mythology, however, we don't necessarily wind up face down in the gutter. Most of us just continue to function and plod along after we bottom out, just as our financial systems continue to function and plod along after each market crash. Soon enough, however, the same addictive cycle begins again, this time under somewhat revised circumstances with new rules and regulations to help prevent the next inevitable crash. But the same addictions remain intact and begin to exert themselves anew.

As addicts in the Great Age of Mediation we are consigned to bottom out numerous times throughout our lives as our addictive cycles repeat themselves over and over and incur more and more complex and expensive prophylactic responses.

The unmanageable complexity of personal and institutional life in the Great Age of Mediation eventually manifests as impenetrable inertia – precisely what makes addictions so very difficult to bust and precisely why meaningful and deliberate change in the 21st century is so excruciatingly slow and difficult. Our microprocessors can crunch millions of calculations per second but as addicts we can no longer bust through our own inertia and change our own lives.

Unaccountability

Addicts are notoriously unaccountable to themselves and others, especially the ones we love the most. Likewise, it's increasingly difficult not to notice the distinct dearth of personal and institutional accountability that follows each major optimized failure. But how can we expect otherwise? Modern systems and institutions are simply so massive and so complex that entropy within them cannot be measured, the precise point of system failure cannot be predicted, and no amount of forensic investigation after the fact can establish any meaningful chain of custody or assign appropriate blame for failure. Just as well, one might suppose, because there seems to be no corresponding political will to assign blame, especially not among the many elected representatives and government agencies whose collective job it is to prevent such runaway calamity in the first place. Accountability in the Great Age of Mediation has effectively been transformed from a reward for good performance into something punitive, a promise of punishment to be avoided at all costs.

In the Great Age of Mediation all calamities aided and abetted by optimized failure are unaccountable by design.

The same systemic unaccountability directly benefits the biggest power players, private and public alike, those who commission, build, sell, deploy, regulate and use the biggest systems. Typically, each successive optimized failure only increases their power and size.

The further consolidation of institutional power among those who already have it and the eradication of accountability are perhaps the most insidious and potentially destructive social byproducts of our super-addiction to all things media and all things digital.

The systemic corporate players declared too big to fail back in 2007 and 2008 are in fact much bigger, much more powerful and much less accountable today, as are the government agencies – old and new alike – ostensibly empowered to regulate them.

One might be forgiven, however, for thinking that the passage of new laws and the expansion of powers granted to regulatory agencies after each optimized failure will somehow prevent the same mischief and abuse the next time, but the exact opposite is true. How can it be otherwise when the regulatory agencies are all populated, managed and advised by ex-employees or future employees of the same industries and corporations they regulate? Apparently, old loyalties and new career ambitions die hard. Working in a senior capacity for the government is a legitimate career path to industry power just as working in a senior capacity for private industry is a legitimate career path to political power. Of course, both are legitimate paths to academic power.

The relationships between the biggest industry players and the biggest government players and the biggest academic players are entirely and unashamedly incestuous, and each successive optimized failure only enriches and empowers them all – corporate, government and academic alike.

Each successive optimized failure consolidates their power and renders them increasingly unaccountable by design – while everyone else gets screwed.

Of course, not all systems break down in such spectacular fashion, just as all addicts don't always bottom out. Optimized failure doesn't always manifest as dramatic denouement; it sometimes just plods along as impenetrable bureaucratic inertia – exactly why more and more laws are enacted and compelled by executive fiat. Public scrutiny – to the extent it still exists at all in the Great Age of Mediation – is replaced by backroom deals while accountability is shifted from elected officials to unelected municipal, state and federal bureaucrats and buried in policy manuals too heavy to lift. Not as exciting, perhaps, but with the same basic downsides: accountability is still nowhere to be found, the biggest and richest players still get bigger and richer and everyone else still gets screwed.

Unfortunately, no one sober is minding the store and the ones who write the laws that govern our lives are – by far – the biggest addicts.

What's Up is Down and What's Down is Up

Marshall McLuhan once observed that media systems pushed to extreme begin to exert an opposite effect; in essence, they begin to operate in reverse. The same basic truth applies to other systems as well.

In the Great Age of Mediation additional intermediation and regulation added on top of already complex systems can only increase instability, de-

Chapter 7

crease accountability and eventually produce the exact opposite of the desired effect.

Of course our addictions represent perfect examples of what happens to us when we push systems to extreme as the pleasures and benefits we once derived from them suddenly turn against us. Likewise, in the Great Age of Mediation the technologies that once delivered prosperity suddenly begin to disintermediate and impoverish us. The digital technologies of scale that once generated millions of jobs in the 1980s and 90s now eliminate them in even greater numbers as large corporations and small businesses alike struggle to cut costs and increase profits. The media and communications technologies that once informed us and protected our civil liberties suddenly delude us and steal away our privacy and freedom. The miraculous high-tech medicine that cures us kills us off as skyrocketing costs render healthcare unaffordable for tens of millions and iatrogenic disease kills hundreds of thousands each year. The amazing communications technologies that once promised to bring us together suddenly fragment and sequester us.

As the immense systems that govern our lives begin to operate in reverse of our expectations, everything up is suddenly down and everything down is suddenly up.

Carrollian fantasy becomes reality in the Great Age of Mediation. And yet we blindly continue to add layer upon layer of technology to the mix, certain in our folly that the high-tech silver bullets we seek are in there somewhere. We are addicted to all things media and all things digital yet continue to look for salvation in all things media and all things digital – per Einstein's definition of insanity – then wonder why we seem to be moving backwards. We spend hours every day and every night immersed in our smartphones and tablets and wonder why we have no time for the important people and things in our lives and why the quality of our lives is slipping away.

Addiction as Moderator

Like most other big lies, the ones that suggest that organized religion is the enemy of all things socially progressive and that every problem has a digital solution didn't just materialize from thin air. Big lies require equally big and pervasive delivery systems. Big lies these days are bought and paid for by big interests, government bodies not least, and are delivered directly by big media – perhaps the biggest of all big interests in the Great Age of Mediation.

Enter 24/7 cable news. The rapid ascent and dominance of 24/7 cable news was the result of a concerted push by global media interests in the 1980s and 90s.

> *As a commercial model, cable news was designed specifically to polarize the audience and create over time a perpetually overheated political environment conducive to the sale of political campaign and special-interest advertising – billions of dollars with each campaign cycle.*

Almost needless to say, there was no consumer demand whatsoever for 24/7 news, just as there was never any consumer demand for 64-ounce soft drinks or drugs that treat restless leg syndrome. In fact...

> *almost all consumer demand in the Great Age of Mediation is entirely manufactured by the marketing and advertising proxies of institutional interests and sold to consumers as part of the Big Lie, essentially to help us confuse freedom of choice for the real thing – the freedom not to participate – and keep us coming back for more.*

Where the news departments of the major broadcast networks traditionally lost money hand-over-fist, the new cable counterparts repurposed the exact same news and made it commercially viable by converting it into entertainment – a far more suitable product for TV. In the process, the broadcast journalists were themselves changed from journalists into entertainers. Many of the more popular cable news personalities who now pose as journalists are in fact barely concealed entertainers paid to promote and exaggerate their political and personality differences on the air. That's why the political news stories with the most legs in the Great Age of Mediation are almost always more about the colorful media personalities who cover them and the perceived biases they bring to their jobs than the more mundane politicians, campaigns and issues themselves. It's also why comedian Jon Stewart is identified as the most trusted journalist in America, and why every scandal-deposed politician, race-baiter and muckraker in the country eventually winds up with a cable news program. Bottom line: issues don't sell but personality and scandals do. The same headlines that once drove newspaper sales don't drive TV news because TV doesn't sell news; TV sells entertainment.

It may help to remember that each communications medium in our lives comes with specific built-in biases that have little in common with the partisan media bias described by the cable news buffoons on either side of the political aisle. Print media, for instance, typically promote linear thought and reason, in part because we are compelled to slow down and think in order to consume them. TV, however, promotes almost pure emotional response and leaves little if any time for contemplative thought. TV makes us feel more than think – precisely why television is such a great medium for commercial advertising, such a great medium for pandering politicians to buy votes and such a lousy medium to produce an informed electorate. Commercial advertisers, politicians and their handlers know that people buy and vote with their hearts and guts, not with their heads.

> *Indeed, just about everything that passes as political debate in the Great Age of Mediation is designed to advance the interests of our super-addiction to all things media and all things digital. The endless media bias, red-state/blue-state, and campaign reform debates are evergreen media inventions designed explicitly to polarize, isolate and sell us more media.*

In truth, the only functional difference between red states and blues states is this: the red states are full of media addicts who consume commercial media all day every day and the blue states are full of media addicts who not only consume commercial media all day every day but also produce all the commercial media that everyone consumes all day every day. Meanwhile, the Tea Party blames the scoundrels in government while Occupy Wall Street blames the scoundrels on Wall Street, yet the scoundrels on Wall Street and the scoundrels on K Street and the scoundrels in Congress and the scoundrels in the White House are all the same scoundrels at different stages of their careers.

Wall Street and Washington, D.C. are entirely synonymous in the Great Age of Mediation. Only the media suggest otherwise, and only as an evergreen foil to sell more media and divert attention away from the fact that power at the top is always incestuous. Only our addiction to media would have us believe that the best way to reform campaign finance is to legislate who can give how much money to whom and on what terms, when what really matters in any political campaign is not where the money comes from but where the money goes, how it's spent and what influence it ultimately buys. And these days political contributions – regardless of affiliation – almost always wind up in the exact same place: in the very deep pockets of very large media corporations. But because everything up is down and everything down is up in the Great Age of Mediation, the real function of campaign finance reform within the media ecosphere is not to ensure fair elections as promoted but to sell more political and special-interest advertising, plain and simple.

Very little of what passes for reasoned debate in the media is what it seems, and all of it is what hap-

pens when the addiction takes over as moderator of the debate.

The medium is very much the message and we are very much addicted to the medium. We turn away from and reject the prophets of moderation and restraint – few of whom can be found on cable TV – while we surrender ourselves to a wildly seductive but ultimately suicidal digital saturnalia. In the Great Age of Mediation we sacrifice our democracy on the altar of easy-access entertainment and trivia.

The Roman historian Livy (59 B.C. –A.D. 17) was a good deal more direct when he wrote about the rise of decadence throughout the empire: "Of late years wealth has made us greedy, and self-indulgence has brought us, through every form of sensual excess, to be, if I may so put it, in love with death both individual and collective." One can only wonder what Livy would have to say about the Great Age of Mediation two millennia later.

Personal Isolation and the Rise of Anti-Social Behavior

In theory, social media and our digital communications tools give us the technological wherewithal to reach out like never before. In practice, however, our addiction to the media – especially our addiction to social media – behaves like every other addiction to every other narcotic and isolates us instead. Our social media technologies turn against us as we push them to extreme, and we withdraw – ironically but inevitably – deeper and deeper into ourselves.

While we have the technological ability to network with and engage more and more people, we typically circumscribe our personal networks to and spend time with those who already share our interests and passions.

In the Great Age of Mediation we wind up perpetually preaching to our own choirs, hermetically sealed off from and wary of any thoughts or passions that don't precisely coincide with our own.

The same basic social phenomenon occurs with us as addicts: as addicts we engage with and confine ourselves to those who share the same addictions. Opium dens, crack houses, bars, adult emporiums, and digital social networks and communities are each full of addicts who all share the same addictions and self-serving ritual behaviors. Indeed, the expressed intent of each acting-out venue – real or virtual – is to facilitate the addiction and provide safe harbor for our addicted behaviors by confining us to our own company and isolating us from outside intervention.

Eventually, our obsessions and addictions seal us off from the rest of the world, despite the siren allure of a global village – certainly among the Great Age of Mediation's most cynical broken promises.

At a certain point in the escalation of our addiction to media, our vastly accelerated technological ability to inspire and accrue so many virtual relationships of all kinds, personal and professional, simply overwhelms us, turns against us and – predictably – begins to operate in reverse.

We discover that our paltry human bandwidth simply cannot accommodate the immense flow of data rushing at us from every conceivable direction – precisely why and when we begin to deploy the very same communications tools that we use to build our virtual networks in a different capacity altogether: we suddenly rely on them to effectively shut down communications instead.

This explains why it's almost impossible these days to just pick up the phone and speak to someone at a large company or government agency without first wading through a labyrinth of endless voice menus (none of which seem to offer the one option we need at the time), even as the recorded voice at the other end professes an abiding passion for excellent customer service.

All of these large institutions are compelled to use their communications technologies as tools to arbitrage the immense, otherwise paralyzing flow of data in and out of their organizations. In essence, they are compelled by their own size and scale to seal themselves off at a certain level from the rest of the world. When almost all correspondence is rendered faceless and skinless, however, the net effect is to further remove and insulate the highest levels of management from any real accountability for their decisions or from any real contact with their own customers or constituents.

Like our institutional counterparts, each of us as individuals is compelled to spend more and more time fending off more and more data, personal and institutional alike. We spend more and more time deciding who we don't want to have relationships with, more and more time deflecting the unsolicited entreaties of the thousands of individuals and institutions who now – thanks to the reckless and promiscuous online behaviors promoted by digital marketers and social media – often have access to the most intimate details of our lives.

Indeed, the ability to dismiss people from our lives with the click of a mouse is the true unspoken appeal of most social media.

Whatever benefits might accrue when like-minded strangers stumble across our social media pages are functionally secondary to the more atavistic and tribal desire to keep strangers out and establish a private online sanctuary for ourselves where we can feel in control of our lives in a patently out-of-control digital world – precisely why the first thing we do with every new social media account is to set permissions and decide who to exclude. And while our desire to exclude others is by no means a bad trait on its own merits or when used in moderation, it changes when it reaches a certain scale and begins to operate in reverse. As the volume of communications increase we spend more and more time each day deciding who we don't want to talk to.

The real intent of all commercial media – social media especially – is decidedly asocial because the real function of commercial media is to isolate us as consumers and cull us from the herd so predatory brands can target, stun and pick us off one by one in the ether.

Social media are a marketing euphemism that represents the end state of a trillion-dollar investment in a seamless user interface designed to eliminate friction and move people online from one virtual place to another virtual place as quickly and profitably as possible. As such, social media are the logical extensions of a commercial on-demand advertising model designed to isolate us as individuals; it's where we wind up when we're constantly en route to me, myself and I – exactly where addicts always wind up.

Social media are the opium dens of the 21st century, where we act out with others addicted to social media.

Thus, while our digital tools empower us to reach out to others, our addiction to them takes over and we retreat more into ourselves in the process. This retreat into ourselves is very much a typical function of addiction. Meanwhile, we are raising a generation of children whose social worlds and communications skills are defined almost entirely by the digital tools and HDTV screens in their hands. As parents we can no longer send kids to their rooms as punishment because their rooms are precisely where they want to be sent – so they can be alone with their immensely amusing digital toys. A more fitting punishment in these Carrollian times would be to send them outside in the fresh air to play with their friends. And while we cannot expect them to do what we say, we can and should expect them to do as we do: they watch us behave like addicts and they model our behavior.

Through our super-addiction to all things media and all things digital we have fashioned for ourselves a society in which most of our waking time is filled with addiction-induced fear, distrust, envy, and shame – the functional calling cards of all commercial media (more about that in the next chapter).

All of the formerly moderating influences and institutions in our lives – things like family, community, and religion – are now under sustained and crippling attack by a massive addiction whose only imperative is pure carpe diem, unfettered consumption of and entitlement to everything right now, especially more media.

Those attributes – faith, deferred gratification, humility and personal sacrifice – that we once viewed as vital contributors to the quality of our lives and communities we still pay lip service to but increasingly regard as naïve, irrelevant, and passé, at least if our behavior is any indication. We hardly notice their absence, in part because there can be no profanity once everything has been rendered profane, and in part because we set no time aside to consider or mourn the demise of quality in our lives.

Chapter 8
Emotional decline in the Great Age of Mediation...

We are wired to seek pleasure and avoid pain – precisely why addiction is such a perfectly normal response mechanism in a society where the pursuit of happiness is the primary call to action, and where modern life in the Great Age of Mediation is so intense and relentless. Yet despite the tsunami of entertainment options in our lives, and despite our endless appetites for them, the eternal optimism that once characterized American society is being severely tested in the Great Age of Mediation. And understandably so: the actual quality of life in America is eroding right before our eyes as our super-addiction to all things media and all things digital consolidates its power over us.

We know, for instance, that the American middle class is being systematically impoverished and disemboweled; real wages and the value of the dollar have been in steady decline for several decades already. We know also that as parents we can no longer realistically expect our children to attain a standard of living higher than our own, and that we

Chapter 8

can no longer expect to afford the requisite higher education that will somehow rescue them from a life of financial struggle and hardship. We know not to expect salvation from any of our institutions or politicians, almost all of whom profess an abiding love and respect for the American middle class (and middle-class values) but more typically work to destroy it while they enrich themselves and the special interests who buy their loyalties for pennies on the dollar. We know that our civil liberties are under attack from the very digital technologies we deploy to protect us from those who would do us harm. We know – deep down in our heart of hearts – that we are complicit in our own addictions, and that our own culture of mass consumption ultimately betrays our core values. Finally and most sadly, those of us old enough to know better know also that the American dream – at least as we've defined it since the end of World War II – is mostly behind us.

All of these things we know, and – per the sober observations of King Solomon three millennia ago – the knowledge of all these things makes us increasingly miserable and dissatisfied. We feel disempowered and betrayed by our own institutions, and wake up one morning to discover that all of our gods have clay feet. We wake up to discover that our technologies in the Great Age of Mediation have begun to turn against us, despite our best efforts and best intentions. We wake up to discover that the entire modern world has been made small by necessity. Everything in it now needs to fit on the little HDTV screens we carry in our pockets, all so we can access a quick fix whenever we feel anxious in the Great Age of Mediation, every few minutes on average – by design.

We wake up one morning to discover that the Great Age of Mediation has given birth to a Great Age of Diminished Expectations.

It seems like the more intermediary channels and technologies we introduce between ourselves and others in the Great Age of Mediation, the more dissatisfied we become with each engagement, and the more we are compelled emotionally to compensate for the lack of quality with increased quantity. But how can it be otherwise when every new communications technology forces us to truncate our emotions and fit them into ever-smaller messages? How can it be otherwise when the volume of smartphone text messages surpasses the number of actual phone calls? How can it be otherwise when our smartphones effectively obliterate the once sacrosanct distinction between our work and personal lives? How can it be otherwise when each new communications technology moves us a notch farther down the *Emotional Impact Ladder*?

Each rung down the *Emotional Impact Ladder* strips additional emotional impact from our communications and increases the volume of communications, as the graphic below illustrates…

Chapter 8

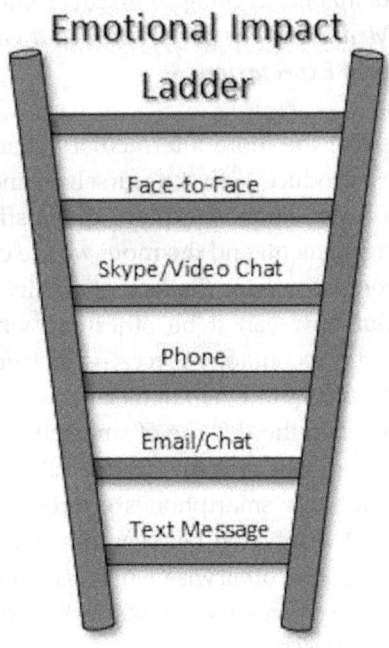

Our investments in time and emotion per communication drop as we descend the *Emotional Impact Ladder*. Per the graph below, we become more emotionally disengaged as we spend more and more time with the communications tools farther down the *Emotional Impact Ladder* – even as the sheer quantity of communications explodes.

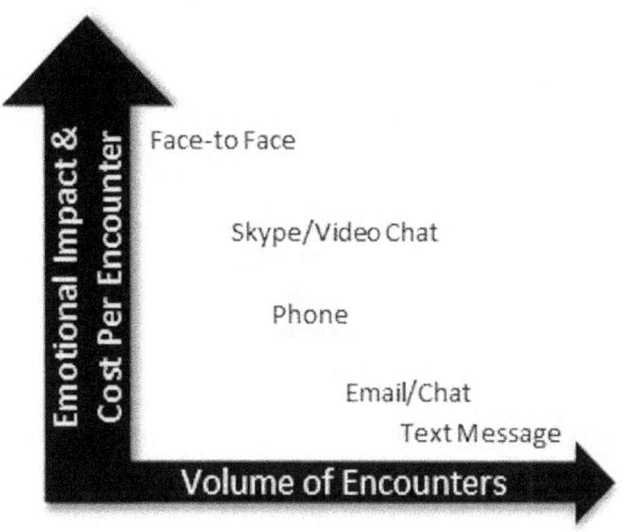

Not coincidentally, the communication tools on the top rungs of the *Emotional Impact Ladder* are the most expensive and time-consuming to invoke, both personally and professionally. But as office productivity tools first and foremost, our laptops and smartphones were designed to drive communications cost-per-engagement down and drive the volume of communications up.

The natural bias of our communications technologies, therefore, is to depersonalize our communications and truncate the higher cost of our emotions while they increase volume.

The more we use our smartphones as everything except a phone, the less emotionally impactful our communications

Chapter 8

become. Meanwhile, the satisfaction-to-volume ratio of our communications declines while our dissatisfaction with the quality of our lives increases. Ironically, the more we communicate in the Great Age of Mediation, the less satisfied we feel.

The net effect of our technology-driven descent down the *Emotional Impact Ladder* is to sequester and polarize our emotional responses and create the perfect storm environment for our addiction to all things media and all things digital to prosper. Fear, distrust, envy and shame: such are the driving emotions and byproducts of all commercial media and all addiction, media addiction no less. One morning on a whim, I set aside a mere ten minutes to flip randomly through my cable TV channels and write down the various threats and dangers that the media considered important enough – for whatever reason – to share with me that morning. The following *Short List of Things to Fear and Distrust* emerged...

Short List of Things to Fear and Distrust	
• China	• terrorists
• neighbors	• open borders
• retirement	• closed borders
• incontinence	• religious fanatics
• rogue comets	• illicit drugs
• predatory teachers	• Democrats
• predatory clergy	• global warming
• identity theft	• boredom
• Republicans	• severe weather
• gum disease	• restless leg syndrome

Please bear in mind that the above *Short List of Things to Fear and Distrust* was compiled from a mere ten-minute exposure to cable television. Now remember that the average American consumes almost 12 hours of media each and every day – or about 70 times longer than it took me to compile my *Short List of Things to Fear and Distrust*.

What we aren't taught to fear we are taught to envy instead. Enough is never enough in the Great Age of Mediation – not nearly. We live our lives in constant fear of not enough money, not enough food, not enough sex, not enough education, not enough information, not enough respect, not enough health, not enough peace of mind, and not nearly enough time to acquire all of the above. Fear and envy are charter members of an incestuous emotional cabal that breeds within each of us an illegitimate sense of bottomless deprivation.

In the Great Age of Mediation, we live our lives immersed in the perception of overwhelming deprivation while we drown in a sea of excess brought into our lives from every conceivable direction by the digital devices in the palms of our hands.

Perhaps what we fear most in the Great Age of Mediation is being alone. Our super-addiction to all things media and all things digital keeps us in a state of perpetual distraction, and flattens our day-to-day emotional reactions to other people and events in our lives. We no longer feel the need to know or learn how to be alone because the little screen gods in our hands tell us we never are. But the ability to be alone with and sort through our own emotions in difficult times is

Chapter 8

a critical conversancy. For some of us, the sudden intrusion of existential aloneness in our lives – for whatever reason – is too devastating to bear, and we find ourselves woefully ill-prepared to deal with the emptiness and pain it brings. A generation ago suicide was a private affair in a basement. But in the Great Age of Mediation, suicide takes out entire schools. In the Great Age of Mediation suicide notes morph into stage productions with entire supporting casts. And it's because everything in our lives plays out on the screens in front of us in high definition. Why shouldn't our own deaths be every bit as dramatic and newsworthy?

Our super-addiction to all things media and all things digital breeds what recovering addicts call *stinking thinking*, the emotional backbone of all addiction and – not coincidentally – the driving emotional force behind all commercial media.

According to our media addiction, the only possible remedy for or protection against all of the stinking thinking in our lives – all of the fear and distrust and envy and shame and anger – is the consumption of even more media. It's the exact same generic prescription offered by all our addictions, regardless of the narcotic: All we ever really need is the very next fix. Our super-addiction to all things media and all things digital promises to provide solutions for any and every problem, especially boredom. Regardless of the problem, however, every solution offered up by our media addiction begins and ends with more media (stay tuned), just as each addictive cycle begins and ends with a barrage of stinking thinking. All of which leads us back to the question raised in Chapter 4: If the medium is the message, what happens to the message when we become addicted to the medium? Ironically, the answer is found in the title of Chapter 3.

The message in all addiction, regardless of the narcotic, is always the same: Eat all you want, we'll make more.

Indeed, more is the only conceivable response to the impoverishment of stinking thinking in the Great Age of Mediation. Our addiction to media promises everything, but can only deliver more of the same: more media, more sex, more credit, more gambling, more fast food, more prescription drugs, more liquor, more tobacco, and more stinking thinking.

In the Great Age of Mediation we've quite naturally handed the entire War Against Drugs over to the biggest dealers on the block – in true Carrollian fashion.

Like all addictions our super-addiction to all things media and all things digital relies on our willingness to dismiss its power. It wants us to think that we are somehow in control of our media consumption habits, when the exact opposite is true:

Each additional technology designed (ostensibly) to help us control and manage the commercial media in our lives – everything from TV remote controls to VCRs to DVRs to apps for our smartphones and tablets – has only increased the amount of commercial media we consume.

And while we are certainly responsible for them, we hardly control them. Indeed, like all late-stage addictions they control us, at least if the current value exchange – what we get in return for the time and money that we invest in them – is any indication. Because all indications in the Great Age of Mediation are that we consistently sell ourselves short; we sell ourselves cheap. But that's what addicts do: they sell themselves cheap for the next fix.

Chapter 9
Physical demise in the Great Age of Mediation...

> *"Man with all his noble qualities...with his godlike intellect which has penetrated into the movement and constitution of the solar system...still bears in his bodily frame the indelible stamp of his lowly origin."*
> – Charles Darwin

Darwin had it right but he may have had it backwards: instead of evolving from apes we may be evolving into apes. With any luck we might find ourselves in another five million years down the evolutionary road perched high atop the jungle canopy with a great view and a fruit platter...

At the end of the day there are few if any desires more profound than those for good health, physical stimulation, general comfort, and – most important among our best wishes – freedom from pain. Freedom from pain is the freedom to think about anything else. Freedom from pain is also the freedom to pursue pleasure. And of course freedom from pain and the pursuit of pleasure (happiness) are the flip sides of the same coin that attracts immigrants to America by the millions. Not coincidentally, freedom from pain and the pursuit of pleasure are also the flip sides of addiction.

The physical downsides of our super-addiction to all things media and all things digital in the Great Age of Mediation hardly need much explanation. The evidence is everywhere we look: epidemic levels of obesity and lifestyle-related degenerative diseases like cancer, diabetes and arthritis, not to mention the massive expansion of the pharmaceutical industry and corresponding abuse of prescription drugs across virtually all social demographics.

In the Great Age of Mediation it seems like the more we know about our own health and finances – at least the more we learn from the commercial media in our lives – the sicker and fatter and poorer we become.

One might assume that with all the information about health and healthcare and money and finance at our fingertips we might be at least a little healthier and at least a little wealthier. But the exact opposite is true: We're sicker and fatter and poorer instead. The more healthy recipes and health tips we consume in the media, the sicker and fatter we become. Likewise, the more financial and money management information we consume in the media, the poorer we become.

The cautions and warnings we hear on TV from well-meaning and well-informed doctors and healthcare professionals simply cannot compete with the sheer emotional impact of 24/7 food channels and tens of billions of dollars of food-related advertising and marketing. Nor can the advice bestowed upon us ad nauseum by the money managers and financial experts who scream at us on cable TV in any way compete with the far more visceral commercial tonnage and economic realities that compel us to spend every dime we make and every dime we can borrow. So we become sicker and fatter and poorer instead – not in spite of our addiction to all things media and all things digital, but precisely because of it. As irrational beings in the Great Age of Mediation we act not in accordance with what we know, but in accordance with the dictates of our obsessive-compulsive behaviors and addictions. We behave like addicts and wonder at the end of the day what happened to our health and money and freedom.

In the Great Age of Mediation the American dinner table of the 1950s has been replaced by on-demand TV everywhere and a convenience food industry designed to accommodate and feed our media addiction, first and foremost. Most of the frozen and microwave foods we eat these days are designed to be eaten while we consume media. Turns out, however, that the more we tailor our eating habits to accommodate our addiction to all things media and all things digital, the sicker and fatter we become, no matter what we eat. Turns out that our waistlines merely expand to accommodate our greater appetites for all things media and all things digital.

Chapter 9

Turns out that we are not what we eat nearly as much as we are how we eat.

Of course, living with addiction of any sort is extremely stressful, and stress is the great killer in the Great Age of Mediation. The mere discrepancy between what we know about our own health and our own unhealthy behaviors generates enormous emotional and physical stress. We know what's good for us yet we consistently behave otherwise. Every smoker chooses to ignore the Surgeon General's warning 20 times for every pack of cigarettes, just as every compulsive eater chooses to ignore the nutrition label on every pack of potato chips and every box of cookies. We know we spend way too much time and money on our addiction to all things media and all things digital, yet we continue to tune in to our smartphones every few seconds and continue to tune out just about everything else in the process – including and especially our health.

The addictions in our lives are difficult to bust precisely because of the massive inertia they generate. Like all addictions, our super-addiction to all things media and all things digital is all about resistance to change and maintenance of the status quo. But persistent and protracted failure to compel change in our own lives – despite what we know – is spiritually, emotionally and physically debilitating. Over time we come to think of ourselves as impotent and incapable of changing our own lives in an endless cycle of self-fulfilling prophecy. We become increasingly inert and moribund – all of which douse the spiritual and emotional fires within us and translates into additional physical stress and anxiety. The additional stress and anxiety contribute in turn to elevated rates of lifestyle-related degenerative disease. Elevated rates of lifestyle-related degenerative disease in our lives produce yet more anxiety and still more stress. The same cycle repeats itself over and over again ad infinitum as any hope for meaningful change fades in the exchange.

Lip service to the contrary notwithstanding, we clearly care less about our health than we do about satisfying the momentary cravings of our super-addiction to all things media and all things digital.

Our addicted lifestyle is almost purely palliative and expedience-based, the exact opposite of preventive.

As a society we have chosen to take a pill to soothe our heartburn after we eat way too much way too fast rather than prevent it by eating more sensibly in the first place. It's not for nothing that the antacid commercial follows the fast food commercial time and time again. Of course, commonsense alternatives like prevention take a backseat to excess once addiction takes over as moderator of all our internal debates. And again, no one ever got rich by selling less of anything. The American healthcare industry in recent years has become the catch-all dumpster for all of our addiction-driven excess. No wonder healthcare costs are so intractable: it's time to pay the piper. The unfortunate truth is that we can't hope to reform American healthcare in any meaningful sense until we first reform our own obsessive-compulsive behaviors. And we cannot hope to reform healthcare as long as the reform debate remains ensconced in and driven by the media. The reason is simple: the politicians and media buffoons who argue healthcare and financial reform and everything else are the biggest addicts, bar none.

Part III

The Quality of Life
Redeemed

Chapter 10
You can intervene on me...

What begins as a trickle ends in a flood, and we will be renewed by the transforming of our minds and spirits. That said, it's obviously far too late to prevent endemic media addiction in 21st-century America; obsessive-compulsive behavior and addiction are already the default conditions. We already spend almost all of our waking time in the act of consuming media, and there are few if any indications that we have learned as a society how to moderate or otherwise regulate our insatiable appetite for all things media and all things digital. Indeed, all of the media consumption statistics indicate the exact opposite, and all of the technologies designed to help us control or personalize our media consumption – including the remote control, the VCR, downloadable music and video, the DVR and on-demand video apps for our portable digital devices – have so far only increased it.

Clearly, our addiction to media is still growing, and has yet to plateau. And while we probably shouldn't expect to see any *just say no to media* public service announcements on television anytime soon, we can however make the choice to change our behavior and improve the quality of life for ourselves and our families today, right here and right now. In fact, this little book in your hands indicates that you have already decided to make that choice. By doing so, you proclaim your optimism for the future and pronounce your faith in change as well.

As some of you doubtless already know, most mainstream addiction recovery programs in this country, including almost all 12-step programs, stress abstinence as the key to recovery. But what you may not know – and doubtless won't learn from the same mainstream addiction recovery programs – is that abstinence is historically and statistically an ineffective strategy against addiction. Think about it: If we could abstain we likely wouldn't become addicts in the first place, and we certainly wouldn't wake up one morning to find ourselves in the Great Age of Mediation. The indisputable fact, however, is that we can't abstain very well at all, despite any pretense or allusion to the contrary. We can hardly even discuss abstinence without exposing our own rank hypocrisy. Consequently, we are thoroughly immersed and entrenched in our own media consumption habits, morning, noon, and night. The media are everywhere we look, and in the very air we breathe. Abstinence is simply not a very viable option in the Great Age of Mediation.

That leaves moderation. But where do we begin? How do we begin the process of replacing our self-serving rituals with more meaningful rituals? Where do we start?

The statistical good news is that most addicts recover from or learn to live with their addictions without professional intervention or help.

Moreover, almost every successful addiction recovery – with or without professional help – works essentially the same way: We learn how to replace the self-serving rituals and stinking thinking of our addictions with more meaningful rituals and more productive and life-enhancing ways to think about ourselves and our world, a process that moderates our behavior over time and improves the quality of our lives by definition.

Each moment devoted to meaningful ritual is one more moment stolen from the stinking thinking of self-serving ritual.

Before we can begin to replace self-serving ritual with more meaningful ritual, however, we must first find a way to disrupt the rhythm of the addiction itself. We must disrupt the addictive cycle. That's why recovery almost always begins with an intervention of some sort, sometimes self-imposed, but far more often compelled by one or more outside agents: a spouse, family member, employer, friend, or court order. Intervention is typically portrayed as the overture to the recovery process, but in fact the entire recovery process is punctuated by ongoing, persistent intervention while the addict learns to replace the self-serving rituals of addiction with more meaningful ritual over time.

As recovering addicts, we learn exactly how and when to intervene in the addiction process; we learn how to trun-

Chapter 10

cate and modify our own stinking thinking, hopefully before it manifests in more self-serving ritual. Instead of hitting the bar after work, for instance, recovering alcoholics might choose to phone a sponsor or attend an AA meeting instead. The phone calls and the meetings simply represent more meaningful and life-affirming replacement rituals for the self-serving rituals of alcoholism. Likewise, the nicotine addict might choose to take a walk and get some fresh air instead of lighting up another cigarette.

The same recovery mechanics are at work, over and over again, often many times daily, regardless of the narcotic: First we find a way to intervene in and disrupt the addictive cycle, then we effectively replace a self-serving ritual with a more meaningful one.

Intervention and recovery, therefore, are entirely conscious acts that require consistently elevated levels of awareness, vigilance, and gratitude. By any metric, addiction recovery is a difficult and demanding process imposed on top of what is likely an already difficult and increasingly unmanageable lifestyle – just one more reason why all addictions are so tough to beat, and why most addicts fail several times before they succeed, if they succeed at all.

As with many things in life, however, relentless persistence is the only true predictor of success.

The following chapters will show you how to intervene gently and appropriately in your own life, how to replace your self-serving rituals with more meaningful ritual, and how to improve your life spiritually, socially, emotionally and physically in the process. They will not show you how to abstain from the media, nor will they show you how to eliminate the media from your life. Rather, they will seek to re-introduce a measure of sobriety amidst the daily cacophony and stress we find in the Great Age of Mediation. They will improve the quality of your life.

122

Chapter 11
The Human Centrifuge...

I remember childhood trips with my father to the Fun House at Playland-at-the-Beach in San Francisco some forty-five years ago. I remember the carnival lights, sounds, smells, and flavors like they happened yesterday – still vivid and visceral. I remember the salt air, sharp and sweet, and how little scrap piles of kelp sometimes washed up on shore and glistened in the midday summer sun like an amber necklace along Ocean Beach. I remember the damp and piercing chill of the late afternoon fog as it rolled through, and the distant roar of the Pacific just across the asphalt ribbons of the Great Highway. I remember Laughing Sal, a female mechanical clown whose grotesque visage and cackling laugh presided over the entrance to the Fun House for decades. I remember how my father's eyes widened when he saw her, and how his face brightened, the slumbering child inside him suddenly reawakened and ready to play.

And I remember one Fun House ride in particular: the human centrifuge, a huge wooden turntable that hovered just an inch or two above a worn padded floor. I remember

Chapter 11

how we all scrambled aboard and plastered ourselves to the great polished disk like animated frescoes, chattering in anxious anticipation. I remember the hum as the motor came alive beneath us and the wheel started to turn, slowly at first, then accelerating, faster and faster until those still clinging to it in extremis suddenly flew off in all directions – screaming in delight. And of course, no one got hurt...

Fade out and fade in, now forty-five years later: Playland-at-the-Beach in San Francisco is gone, long ago demolished and auctioned off, replaced by rows of non-descript seaside condominiums. Some things remain, however: the roar of the Pacific, Ocean Beach, the Great Highway, the fog, the chill, the salt air and, of course, the memories. Forty-five years later it occurs to me that life in the early 21st-century is very much like the human centrifuge ride of my childhood, very much like the spinning wheel in the Fun House at Playland-at-the-Beach. My human centrifuge, however, runs 24/7, day after day, month after month, year after year. It never stops. It never even slows down. In fact, it accelerates with each revolution. The centrifugal force and inertia we encounter on it continually increase, and there's no padding to break your fall if you get tossed off; everyone who gets tossed off gets hurt. Welcome to modern life in the Great Age of Mediation.

It's time to introduce you to the *Centrifugal Map*. A graphic representation follows...

The Centrifugal Map

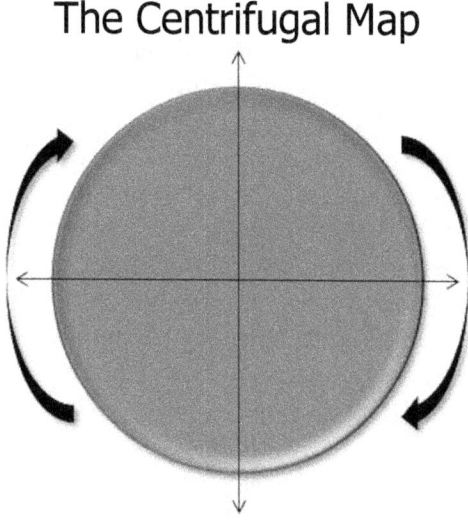

The big black arrows on either side of the *Centrifugal Map* represent the fact that the human centrifuge is always spinning, while the thin lines that bisect the wheel horizontally and vertically represent the centrifugal force exerted outward in all directions by the spinning wheel. To properly invoke the human centrifuge as a metaphor for modern life, however, we need to consider three things:

1. *The wheel always spins and never slows down for anyone.* Our job is to withstand the centrifugal force and remain on the wheel at all costs. And if we get tossed off, as sometimes happens, we must climb back on again, irrespective of any injuries or scars we may sustain in the process.

2. *In the absence of countervailing forces or actions, we will always drift by default towards the wheel's outer edge in the Great Age of Mediation.* The centrifugal force generated by the human centrifuge is inexorable, and will always act to nudge us outward towards the edge. It therefore doesn't matter which way the wheel turns: clockwise, counterclockwise, liberal, conservative, Democrat, Republican, Christian, Moslem, Jew, Buddhist, or Hindu – the physics that govern the wheel are ordained from above, constant and inviolate.

3. *Where we are on the Centrifugal Map at any given point in time will determine the quality of our lives at that moment, and where we spend most of our time on the wheel will determine the general quality of our lives.* Albert Einstein once observed that the outer edge of a phonograph record spins faster than the hub at the center. The same is true of the human centrifuge and the *Centrifugal Map*: in general, life is better towards the center of the wheel where there is less centrifugal force to battle, and worse towards the outer edge where the centrifugal force is greatest. So not only is it important to stay on the wheel, but also to position yourself as close to the center as possible.

The first two conditions above qualify as *force majeure,* pure acts of God, things over which we exert no control whatsoever – no matter how hard we try. Simply stated, the human centrifuge will always spin, and will always generate centrifugal force outward from the center as a default condition, irrespective of our behavior. Only the third condition – where we position ourselves on the wheel – is subject to our own influence. At any given point in time we will find ourselves positioned on the human centrifuge either closer to the center of the wheel or closer to the wheel's outer edge.

Let's examine how our position on the wheel affects the quality of our lives, starting from the outer edge then working our way inward. Remember while we do so, however, that our lives are works in progress, and that our position on the human centrifuge and *Centrifugal Map* can change from day to day, or even from moment to moment, depending on circumstances and the choices we make.

Life on the Edge of the Human Centrifuge...

As mentioned earlier, the Big Lie promoted to us by our super-addiction to all things media and all things digital in the Great Age of Mediation rightfully interprets our faith as a mortal threat to its own existence, and therefore positions it in our heads as the polar opposite and primary threat to reason. Portrayed graphically on the *Centrifugal Map,* the Big Lie looks like this…

Chapter 11

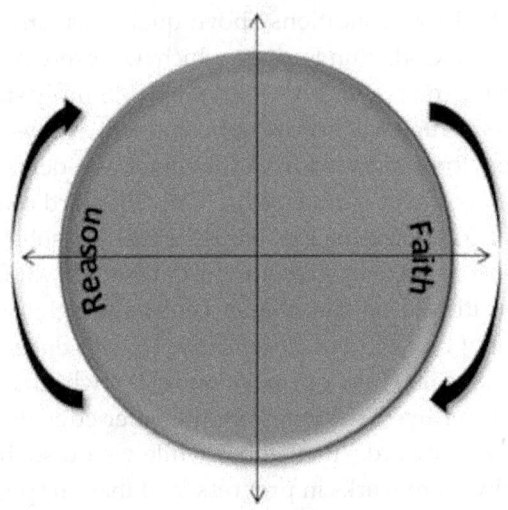

In truth, however, reason and faith belong side by side in the center of the *Centrifugal Map* because faith is a reasonable response to the insanity we encounter in the Great Age of Mediation. Remember, the Big Lie is by definition an extreme position, just as addiction is by definition an extreme condition, and cannot permit any meaningful reconciliation of the two. Such a marriage would threaten to produce a more balanced and moderate lifestyle, something our super-addiction to all things media and all things digital simply cannot and will not tolerate.

All of us spend time (perhaps more than we'd like) on the outer edge of the human centrifuge. Indeed, life on the edge is the default condition in the Great Age of Mediation simply because addiction is the default condition in the Great Age of Mediation. Addiction aside, however, our paths through life are strewn with the bones and roadside markers of lost loved ones, failed businesses, divorce, unemployment, violence, drugs, alcohol and other addictions, financial problems, and legal hassles. These and other Black Swan events rattle our cages, knock us upside the head, and loosen our grip on the wheel. And sometimes – weary from the day-to-day attrition of the battle just to stay on the wheel – we close our eyes to steal a moment or two of blissful quiet, then wake with a start to find ourselves suddenly drifting right back out towards the edge again. Out there, out where the storm winds blow, we have no time to lick our wounds, and simply brace ourselves for the next big gust. But that's life on the edge in the Great Age of Mediation.

Remember, the quality of life is a function of how and where and with whom we invest our time and faith.

In the Great Age of Mediation, most of our time is spent on the edge of the human centrifuge in default reaction to the pressures and demands – the centrifugal force – encountered in an extreme environment.

Little or no time therefore to contemplate right or wrong, little or no time to ponder healthy versus unhealthy or sacred versus profane, and all while our super-addiction to all things media and all things digital tells us – as part of the Big Lie – that our utter obsession with all things media all things digital is not only benign, but a legitimate and reasonable response to the extreme environments we encounter in life on the edge in the Great Age of Mediation.

Extreme begets extreme.

Chapter 11

Life of the edge of the human centrifuge is also where we encounter much more inertia in our lives per the following illustration...

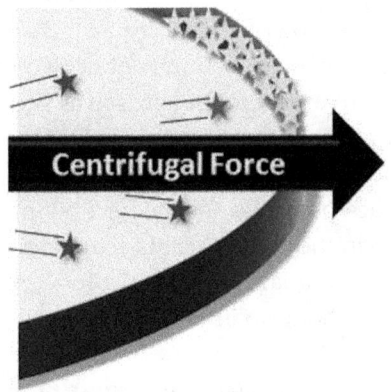

The massive inertia generated by our super-addiction to all things media and all things digital combines with the intense centrifugal force we feel at the edge of the human centrifuge, and together they work to prevent us from moving inward towards the center of the wheel where the quality of life is much better, much more liberated and much less stressful.

> *Life on the edge of the human centrifuge keeps us mired in the stressful minutiae and technology-driven exigencies of day-to-day survival. It demands that we spend nearly all of our time just fighting to stay on the wheel while we struggle to feed and sustain our obsessions and addictions.*

But time and energy devoted to the struggle to feed our obsessions and addictions in life on the edge is time and energy diverted away from and borrowed against the quality of life. And of course we cannot afford to borrow indefinitely; the quality of life – like all credit lines – is finite.

The daily skirmishes and battles with our obsessions and addictions carve the harsh landscape, the rollercoaster ups and downs, of life on the edge in the Great Age of Mediation. As demonstrated earlier, the immense struggle to maintain and support our fealty and addiction to media consumes almost all of our waking time. Of course no amount of talent, money, or good will can improve our position on the human centrifuge in the absence of time – because we simply cannot buy, beg, borrow, or steal any more of it. And therein resides the real dilemma:

In the Great Age of Mediation life on the edge seems full of just about everything except time – and peace of mind.

Ironically, life on the edge is where all of our time is consumed in fealty and addiction to our time-saving digital technologies. Ultimately, however, our obsessions with and addictions to the same time-saving digital technologies imprison and enslave us. Life on the edge in the Great Age of Mediation keeps us thoroughly entertained and thoroughly mesmerized by high-definition and surround-sound technologies wherever and whenever we want them, but thoroughly immersed in the glittering gulags of our own obsessions and addictions. Life on the edge keeps us mired in perpetual crisis management. And unfortunately, life on the edge is precisely where we choose to spend more and more of our time in the Great Age of Mediation.

Life in Transition on the Human Centrifuge...

While we have no choice but to remain on the human centrifuge, we are called upon nevertheless to make the daily choices that – in no small measure – determine our position on it. Free will is a muscle we need to exercise. Functionally, the choices we make – minute by minute, hour by hour, and day by day – either keep us where we are on the human centrifuge, combine with circumstance to move us closer to the outer edge, or combine with circumstance to move us closer to the center.

> *Our predisposition to choose in ways that promote either the quality of life or our obsessions and addictions depends largely on where we are positioned on the wheel at the time we make our choices.*

Obsessive-compulsive behavior aside, we are very much creatures of habit to begin with, and all behaviors – good, bad, and indifferent – become easier with practice. The closer we are to the outer edge, the more likely we are to predicate our choices on convenience rather than quality, and the more likely we are to slip by default into compulsive behaviors that promote or sustain our obsessions and addictions. Out on the edge we are far more likely to react to our environment, and far more likely to make less-considered and ill-informed choices. The longer we live life on the edge, the more difficult it becomes to imagine any other way to live. Protracted exposure to life on the edge inhibits courageous decisions that will help us escape the prison of our addictive behavior and restore the quality of our lives.

Again, it bears repeating that we are almost always in transition on the human centrifuge, almost always moving farther from or closer to the center. Our movement in either direction almost always results from a confluence of circumstance and the choices we make from moment to moment, day to day. Movement in either direction is no guarantee that we will be moving in the same direction five minutes from now.

The only guarantee is that the quality of life will improve as we move towards the center of the human centrifuge, and will deteriorate as we move towards the edge.

Life in the Center of the Human Centrifuge...

Life in the center of the human centrifuge is a fully liberated and wholly conscious life predicated on the deliberate choice of quality over convenience in an environment less compelled and controlled by our obsessions and addictions. Although life in the center of the human centrifuge is antidotal to life on the edge, they are not polar opposites. Indeed, there's nothing whatsoever polar about the quality of life at the center of the human centrifuge. It will always meet you halfway.

Life in the center of the human centrifuge is a conscious balance of faith and reason restored in proportion.

Chapter 11

In fact, the center of the human centrifuge is where we begin our journey in life, born free with free will, and where freedom and free will remain as essential life forces throughout our lives.

The table below summarizes the contrasting lifestyle attributes that characterize life on the edge of the human centrifuge versus life in the center...

Life on the Edge	Life in the Center
- Reactive - Full of inertia - Predicated on quantity - More stressful - Hectic and time-starved - Empty and deprived - Powerless - Victim	- Proactive - Liberated - Predicated on quality - Less stressful - Relaxed and composed - Full and abundant - Powerful - Victor

Take a moment to review the above table once again, then ask yourself: If the quality of my life is a function of how and where and with whom I invest my time and faith, how and where and with whom would I rather invest them?

The choices you make in response to the above question will help determine your position on the human centrifuge. You can move closer to the center and begin to improve the quality of your life right now. It's up to you. Read on...

Chapter 12
Uncommon sense...

"Everybody gets so much information all day long that they lose their common sense." – Gertrude Stein

Once again, the medium is the message: the more we rely and depend upon the ubiquitous HDTV screens in our lives for information about our spiritual, social, emotional and physical well-being, the less compelled we are to rely and act on our own common sense – a far cheaper, more dependable and far less conflicted self-defense mechanism and arbiter of our own behavior. The more third-party information and expertise we introduce between ourselves and our own common sense the sicker and fatter and poorer and less free we become.

Unfortunately, common sense is not something we can afford to ignore for long.

Common sense, like the muscles in our bodies, atrophies with neglect.

Chapter 12

The more we ignore it in pursuit of the convenient and the expedient, the less able we are to invoke it. The more we defer it to the presumed knowledge and advice – however sound and sensible – of commercially conflicted experts who know neither our individual bodies nor our individual finances, the harder it becomes to call upon it when we need it most.

And the more media we consume the more we need common sense. In the Great Age of Mediation the more media we consume the less time we have for everything else, common sense not least. Of course, common sense is a sworn enemy of our super-addiction to all things media and all thing digital – and all other addictions as well – in no small measure because common sense is a moderating agent and would likely suggest that we not consume so much media in the first place.

The Carrollian nature of life in the Great Age of Mediation defies common sense by definition. It's what happens when our addiction takes over as moderator of the debate, and what happens when the institutions and technologies in our lives turn against us and start operating in reverse. Common sense becomes increasingly less common as we rely more and more on media-borne, third-party expertise to mediate and resolve our problems. After all, who needs common sense when every expert on every subject has a TV show, weblog, podcast or online video to parcel on-demand answers and advice 24/7? The common sense we no longer take time to summon from within can always be found somewhere on TV or just a few clicks away online.

Common sense is a victim of our super-addiction to all things media and all things digital in the Great Age of Mediation.

The erosion of common sense results in a life every bit as irrational and nonsensical as some secularists among us might consider a monastic life devoted to God. Of course, as addicts – religious or irreligious – we devote ourselves to a god of a different sort anyway. That said, the distinctions between monastic life and life as an addict in the Great Age of Mediation are clear: Monastic life eschews material comfort; life as an addict in the Great Age of Mediation relies on it. Monastic life is essentially deliberate and contemplative; life as an addict in the Great Age of Mediation is essentially reactive and dismissive. Monastic life finds peace of mind in questions that cannot be answered in a lifetime of asking; life as an addict in the Great Age of Mediation finds nothing but turmoil, anxiety and defeat in any question that can't be resolved by a search engine in a split second. Monastic life is mission-driven and full of meaningful ritual; life as an addict in the Great Age of Mediation is tool-driven and full of self-serving ritual. Those who choose a monastic life follow long-established rules of conduct designed to maintain an ascetic social order and promote a lifestyle of contemplation and meditation in pursuit of existential truth; as addicts in the Great Age of Mediation we are compelled to ignore or break or amend the rules as needed in order to disrupt the social order in pursuit of personal advantage. The rules that govern monastic life are inviolate and are predicated on common sense. The rules that govern life in the Great Age of Mediation are predicated on expedience and are therefore disposable and replaceable as circumstances warrant – common sense be damned. Both lifestyles are essentially irrational but only one is deemed as such. Both are extreme but only one is deemed as such.

Extreme becomes the new normal when addiction takes over as moderator of the debate.

In the Great Age of Mediation common sense is to life on the edge of the human centrifuge what the spotted owl is to the clear-cut forest: virtually nonexistent. In the Great Age of Mediation common sense is entirely uncommon, crowded out of our lives by a super-addiction to all things media and all things digital that tells us the only answer to all our problems is more of everything – especially more media and more digital devices. Common sense requires time to think and space to breathe, neither of which are available to us in life on the edge.

In the Great Age of Mediation common sense is just too inconvenient and too time-consuming to fit into our lives.

Whatever common sense remains to us in the Great Age of Mediation is telling us that more media and more digital firepower at our fingertips are not the answers to anything except the balance sheets of those who produce, sell and distribute more media and more digital devices. Quite the opposite, in fact:

Common sense and the quality of life are both subtractive.

The restoration of common sense and the quality of life in the Great Age of Mediation relies first and foremost on our ability to disintermediate our lives and reduce our slavish reliance on the third-party experts in the media who forever tell us to stay tuned no matter what. More specifically:

The restoration of common sense in our lives and the quality of our lives relies on our ability to do three things: slow down, let go of failure and embark on a course of deliberate simplicity.

Slow Down

"For fast-acting relief try slowing down." – Lily Tomlin

We take antacids for fast relief from fast foods. We make quick deposits at the bank and withdraw quick cash. We stand in the supermarket express lane and hope no one will stop us to count the number of items in our shopping baskets. We heat pre-cooked meals in the microwave and grab snacks on the go. We schedule meetings on the run and send instagrams from our smartphones. We study online to earn accelerated degrees. We fast-track whatever

Chapter 12

we can whenever we can, and much prefer instant to deferred gratification.

Of the many things that sound easy in theory but always prove most difficult in practice, slowing down in the Great Age of Mediation is right at the top of the list. Everyone wants to slow down, but no one can. It just seems like slowing down is anathema to everything we are and everything we do. Everyone wants the time to kick back and enjoy life, but few of us still know how to get from here to there.

It's hard to slow down when everyone and everything around us is speeding up; it just doesn't seem like a rational thing to do. Of course we attach much more significance to rational things than we do to irrational things to begin with, despite the fact that the entire consumer economy is predicated on wholly irrational purchase decisions made at point of sale – a fact well known to all first-year MBAs but immediately forgotten the moment they step into the real world and start drinking their own Kool-Aid. Nevertheless, a trillion-dollar consumer economy suggests that we spend more than a little time each day with our dials set to *irrational*.

Not only do we almost always value rational over irrational thought and behavior, we actively disdain the irrational things that most resist rational explanation. But that may be a function of our super-addiction to all things media and all things digital at work as moderator of the debate. Our addictions may be insane, but they're hardly irrational and – as mentioned way back in Chapter 3 – are perfectly normal and perfectly rational behavioral adaptations to the madness of the world we occupy. Much easier to explain in fact than the irrational relationships and things in our lives that contribute so crucially to the quality of our lives – little things like love and faith and serendipity. Indeed, the same irrational little things – love and faith and serendipity – are the very things that seem to work best as active agents to moderate our entirely rational addicted behaviors. By defining the same irrational relationships and things as pejoratives with no reasonable place in a post-modern world of rational beings engaged in rational behaviors, our super-addiction to all things media and all things digital destroys its only real competition. All the more reason it seems to embrace the irrational things and relationships we can't otherwise explain. All the more reason to embrace love, take a leap of faith and invite serendipity back into our lives.

Our obsessions with productivity, goals and achievement very much reflect our obsessions with our own digital devices and tools, all of which have office pedigrees that not so coincidentally extol the rational virtues of productivity and goals and achievement over irrational things and relationships that can't be explained, measured or quantified.

With all sincerity we tell ourselves and others that we only want our children to be happy, Meanwhile, we extol them to perform in a high-stakes race that begins in pre-school and extends through college.

The more pedestrian and less noble truth is that we would much prefer our children to be successful than happy, at least if the behavior we model for them is any indication.

Chapter 12

We simply no longer believe in our hearts that the green will return to the trees in the spring, and – more importantly – we no longer seem to care, or maybe we're just too busy to care.

Either way, the truth is that we've lost faith in serendipity, the part of us that delights from and welcomes discovery in wrong turns.

But how can we welcome serendipity or take a wrong turn when our mapping technologies always default to the fastest and most direct route? Who can find us and how can we be found if we're never lost in the first place?

Who needs serendipity when we have GPS?

We must find a way to be mindful of how our digital devices and tools accelerate our lives as a default fact of life in the Great Age of Mediation. We must remain mindful of the office pedigree inherent in the digital tools we carry with us as consumer devices everywhere we go, and remember that our lives accelerate in accordance with the speed, power and ubiquity of our tools.

We must also be mindful of our tendency to become our attention. Our behavior begins to mirror the frenetic speed, fragmentation and sheer volume of the media and digital devices we invite into our lives, and we grow increasingly impatient with any problem that cannot be resolved with a few keystrokes. Of course, the number of problems we encounter that cannot be resolved with just a few keystrokes increases along with the complexity of our lives. Our super-addiction to all things media and all things digital compels us to search desperately for the right combination of technology and expertise to improve the quality of our lives at every turn, but the additional technology and expertise we impose on ourselves only compounds our problems. They produce more acceleration and more inertia and more anxiety and more fear as the quality of our lives continues to erode and we sink deeper into our addiction.

My Ritual Inventory in the next chapter will show you precisely how to slow down for a few moments each day without slamming on the brakes and without busting the bank.

Let Go of Failure

"Insanity: doing the same thing over and over again and expecting different results." – Albert Einstein

Many recovering addicts define addiction as a form of insanity, per Einstein's observation above. In the Great Age of Mediation we look over and over again to the experts in the media for advice on how to live better, more productive lives. Better to let someone else handle the problem for us. Better to let someone with the specific knowledge and skills we need take over. Better in the Great Age of Mediation to hand our lives over to experts, to those who media ecologist Neil Postman once referred to as the high priests of *Technopoly*, his name for a society and culture subject to and governed by its own technology.

Chapter 12

Common sense, however, tells us that our increasing reliance on media-driven, third-party expertise isn't working out too well. We have legions of experts telling us precisely how to lead better lives across hundreds of TV channels and millions of websites. Thousands of experts telling us how to improve our health, thousands of experts telling us how to slim down and weigh less, thousands of experts telling us how to improve our finances and thousands of experts dispensing relationship advice.

Yet for all the expert advice we consume virtually every day of our lives in the Great Age of Mediation, we find ourselves sicker, fatter and poorer, with divorce rates that now reflect and predict more failure than success in our personal relationships.

We obviously don't lack for good advice freighted with common sense from qualified experts, experts with advanced degrees from prestigious universities and with years of experience in their fields.

But in the Great Age of Mediation common sense is the proverbial Surgeon General's Warning: it simply doesn't matter to addicts. Addicts could care less about the writing on the wall.

Who cares if every major financial scandal and collapse is engineered by experts with MBAs from top-flight business schools? Who cares if the same media-driven experts who failed to warn us about the market crashes of 1999, 2007 and 2008 are still pitching the same self-serving financial advice harder and louder than ever across hundreds of TV channels and millions of websites? Who cares if the same media-driven congressional leaders who failed to protect the nation from financial calamity for the past three decades are still pandering to the exact same special interests – and enriching themselves in the process? Who cares that our media-driven healthcare system promotes moral hazard and wrecks our health? Who cares that none of the media-driven experts in our lives will predict the next Black Swan event to whack us upside the head? Who cares if our media-driven faith in the media-driven best and brightest among us is tragically misplaced? Who cares about any of the media-driven problems of the world when all that truly matters to media addicts is the next media-driven fix?

Letting go of failure in the Great Age of Mediation means understanding that up is down and down is up. It means we arrive at common sense in spite and not because of our education, in spite and not because of all the advice we find in the media.

Letting go of failure in the Great Age of Mediation means letting go of our reliance on the convenience and spectacle of media-driven expertise – because it simply no longer works. In order to make room for healing agents like common sense and gratitude in our lives we must first subtract something else. As mentioned earlier, the quality of life in the Great Age of Mediation is subtractive, a function of disintermediation.

Chapter 12

We cannot improve the quality of our lives in the Great Age of Mediation unless and until we first slow down long enough to assess our own behavior and let go of what we know doesn't work.

That said, I'm not naïve enough to think for a moment that we can just say no to the media or digital devices in our lives, at least no more than we can with any other addiction to any other highly addictive drug. And we can't just check into a rehab clinic en masse, cleanse ourselves of stinking thinking and re-emerge only to re-immerse ourselves in media once again. But we can begin to examine our behavior and values. When we do we'll discover that...

our super-addiction to all things media and all things digital exists not in spite of our values – as many recovery experts claim – but because of them.

My Ritual Inventory in the next chapter will show you precisely how to examine your behavior and values, how to let go of failure – gently but surely – over time, and how to replace it with behaviors that work for you instead of against you.

Embark on a Path of Deliberate Simplicity

"I would not give a fig for the simplicity this side of complexity, but I would give my life for the simplicity on the other side of complexity."
-- Oliver Wendell Holmes

In the Great Age of Mediation, a time of immense complexity and haste, we need to embark on a deliberate mission to find the simplicity on the other side of complexity. We've pushed the systems in our lives to extreme, and now they've all begun to push back. We are being buried in a landfill full of failed passwords, depleted batteries and the tangled cords of obsolete power adaptors, and we spend half of our unplugged time anxiously searching for places to plug back in.

In the Great Age of Mediation we assume speed and convenience add up to quality in our lives. But that assumption is true only to the extent that we are able somehow to convert the additional speed and convenience at our disposal into more discretionary time to pursue those things that constitute the quality of our lives.

Who among us would choose to pursue complexity over simplicity in the Great Age of Mediation?

Who among us would utter the dying wish to spend more time at the office? But the accelerated pursuit of more speed and more convenience are byproducts of our addiction to the digital devices that clutter our lives.

The inconvenient truth in the Great Age of Mediation is that more speed and more convenience no longer buy us more discretionary time because all of our discretionary time is already consumed by our super-addiction to all things media and all things digital.

Chapter 12

As addicts we no longer pursue the quality of life. As addicts we sacrifice the quality of life for the next fix. As addicts we sacrifice simplicity for unmanageable complexity.

Our addiction-driven pursuit of speed and convenience assumes that a friction-free life is a better life. But that's the addiction talking as moderator over all our internal debates.

In truth, the quality of our lives reflects the deliberate friction we slow down long enough to create for ourselves.

We cannot improve the quality of our lives in the Great Age of Mediation unless and until we first slow down long enough to assess our own behavior, let go of what we know doesn't work and embark on a path of deliberate simplicity. *My Ritual Inventory* in the next chapter will show you exactly how to do all three.

Chapter 13
My Ritual Inventory...

In the previous chapter I explained that the secret to restoring common sense and the quality of our lives resides in our ability to slow down, let go of failure and embark on a path of deliberate simplicity. I'd like to introduce you now to an elegantly simple tool designed to do all three things. Meet *My Ritual Inventory...*

I suggested way back in Chapter 1 that all quality things share three common traits: Quality is a gift, quality imparts meaning, and quality demands our time and attention. We ascribe value to things when we turn our time and attention to them. I then went on to suggest that our appreciation of quality is an act of commission, and as such likewise demands our time. But appreciation is just another word for *gratitude,* and gratitude is the true foundation of all healing and all quality. If we want quality in our lives, we must set aside time to show our gratitude for it.

In his wonderful bestselling book about building wealth, *Secrets of the Millionaire Mind: Mastering the Inner Game of Wealth,* author and lecturer T. Harv Eker says:

Chapter 13

> *"Focus on what you have, not on what you don't have. Make a list of ten things you are grateful for in your life and read the list aloud. Then read it each morning for the next thirty days. If you don't appreciate what you've got, you won't get anymore and you don't need anymore."*

My Ritual Inventory is a simple and proven variation on the theme mentioned by Mr. Eker above. It's about invoking gratitude as the driving component of conscious daily intervention, the first step in the gradual replacement of the self-serving rituals of our super-addiction to all things media and all things digital with more meaningful rituals over time. It's about change that begins as a trickle and becomes a mighty river whose many tributaries and streams make good our lives. It's about squeezing out our stinking thinking one thought at a time, about replacing each stinking thought with one imbued instead with abundance, grace, and gratitude. It's about invoking gratitude as a moderating agent in the Great Age of Mediation, about moving closer to the center of the human centrifuge and farther away from life on the edge. It's about slowing down, letting go of failure and embarking on a path of deliberate simplicity. *My Ritual Inventory* will put first things first each time you invoke it. It will right your thoughts and clear your mind – at least for a little while.

There is indeed nothing new under the sun, and every minute of every day is spent in fealty to and pursuit of one or more of the four basic needs discussed earlier: spiritual, social, emotional and physical. The quality of our lives and the quality of the society we live in is measured in our ability or inability to satisfy them. Our character is revealed through our struggles with them while entire civilizations rise and fall accordingly. Thus has it been for all mankind since the dawn of time, and thus will it remain.

Our exploration of *My Ritual Inventory* begins with a simple definition of meaningful ritual:

Meaningful ritual is any regularly scheduled activity that enhances and promotes one or more of our four basic needs: spiritual, social, emotional or physical.

In practice, the distinctions between self-serving and meaningful rituals are pretty self-evident. For instance, a few quiet minutes spent with a cup of coffee or tea each morning qualifies as meaningful ritual. That same cup of coffee or tea if quaffed in a mad dash out the door does not — even if it happens at the same time every day. Likewise, a morning jog qualifies whereas a frenzied sprint out the door to catch the bus to work doesn't. Dinner with the family around the dinner table qualifies; stuffing your face with a slice of pizza on the run every evening doesn't. By the same measure, any addiction recovery programs attended on a regular basis qualify, whereas the addictive rituals they address do not. Regularly scheduled biweekly or monthly events — such as book club meetings or theater outings — also qualify. Ad hoc gatherings of family or friends don't. Church every Sunday qualifies, but lifting a prayer to your Higher Power at the race track may not, even if you do it every Sunday right after church. Regular work around the yard or tending the garden qualifies, but breaking out the *Weed Whacker* once every two years doesn't. A cigarette with a snifter of brandy after dinner might constitute a perfectly appropriate evening ritual, as long as the cigarette is not one of forty you inhale each day, and as long as the brandy doesn't precede or follow a bottle of gin.

| Table of Meaningful Rituals ||
Category	Meaningful Rituals
Spiritual	worship and prayer, scripture reading, some music, yoga, meditation, volunteer work, some recovery programs
Social	family activities (including meals), music appreciation with friends or family, household chores, sports and games, work, group therapy, volunteer work, some recovery programs
Emotional	therapy, reading, music appreciation, yoga, journal writing, meditation, hobbies, social events with friends, family activities (including meals), household chores, recovery programs
Physical	exercise, participation sports, household chores, yoga, dance, physical therapy, massage, personal grooming, long walks, meditation, cooking, napping, recovery programs

The above *Table of Meaningful Rituals* is offered as a general guideline, and is by no means complete. You may notice, however, that none of the listed rituals – with the sole exception of music appreciation – rely on or revolve around electronic media. For the purposes of the following exercise, those rituals that rely on or revolve around television, the Internet (including email, instant messaging, social networks, and chat), smartphones and video games don't make the cut for now, even if they enhance and promote one or more of your four basic needs per the above definition of meaningful ritual. The only exceptions to the rule are those rituals that revolve around and are specific to making music and/or music appreciation. But don't dismay: You are perfectly free to indulge in all of your current electronic media consumption habits – with no restrictions whatsoever. I ask only that you resist the temptation (however strong) to define and list them as meaningful rituals in the *My Ritual Inventory* exercise that follows.

Let's move on now to the *My Ritual Inventory* worksheet, a working inventory of the meaningful rituals in your life per the above definition. First, make and date a copy of the *My Ritual Inventory Worksheet* on the following page...

My Ritual Inventory Worksheet

Meaningful Ritual	Time per mo	SP	SO	EM	PH
Total minutes					
Total hours					

Now...

1. Begin by listing each of the meaningful rituals in your life that you perform on a regularly scheduled basis (for now, don't include any meaningful ritual with a frequency of less than once a month, and don't include your job). List each qualifying ritual only once, regardless of how frequently you repeat it each week or month.

2. After you have listed each of the meaningful rituals that you perform at least once each month, calculate the time you devote each month to each ritual in minutes and write it down in the *Time per month* column. You may need to keep a calculator handy, and it's probably a good idea to use a pencil instead of a pen.

3. After you have calculated the amount of time you devote to each ritual on a monthly basis, assign how the time you spend with each ritual breaks down across each of the four basic needs, represented in the table headings (SP = Spiritual, SO = Social, EM = Emotional and PH = Physical) per the example table below. (Note: It's perfectly okay for the total amount of time that you assign across all four basic needs to exceed the actual time you devote to the ritual.)

4. Add *My Ritual Inventory* to the end of your worksheet as a separate meaningful ritual, but

don't assign any time figures or basic-need categories.

5. Next, per the example below, add the total minutes for each column in the *Total Minutes* row, then divide each total by sixty to arrive at the total number of hours devoted to the enhancement of each basic need.

My Ritual Inventory Worksheet					
Meaningful Ritual	Time per mo	SP	SO	EM	PH
Prayer walks	120	60	60	60	60
Phone Mike	1200		1200	1200	
Exercise	960				960
Total minutes	2280	60	1260	1260	1020
Total Hours	38	1	21	21	17

In the above example I listed three meaningful rituals, calculated the monthly time I devote to each in minutes, then assigned specific amounts of time to whichever of the four basic needs each ritual enhanced in my life each month. For instance, I take monthly spiritual walks with a small group from my church and community. We gather one Saturday morning every month, pray and share scripture the first hour, then walk for another hour. The total time spent each month with my group prayer walks is about two hours or 120 minutes. Since the first hour of each get together is strictly prayer and scripture, I entered 60 minutes under SP for spiritual. I also assigned 60 minutes to each of the other three basic needs. Please note that the assignment of time is strictly subjective, and will most certainly change as your life circumstances change. Sometimes we modify the rituals themselves, sometimes we simply grow out of them and set them aside, and sometimes we replace them entirely with others.

As noted above, the total time you assign across all of the categories may and often will exceed the actual time you devote to the ritual. For instance, I invest a total of two hours (120 minutes) of actual time each month to my group prayer walks, but I derive four hours (240 minutes) in perceived benefits, twice the amount I actually invest. That's a pretty good return, and that's only one meaningful ritual; it only hints at the power of meaningful ritual to change your life for the better, and the inherent wisdom of quality over quantity. My twenty-hour investment of time on the phone with my brother each month returns forty hours in perceived emotional and social benefits. Again, a pretty good return by any measure, and even better when we consider that each thought and act dedicated to meaningful ritual is another thought and act stolen away from our supply of stinking thinking and self-serving ritual. The benefits of meaningful rituals accrue like compound interest. The mere fact that our investments in meaningful ritual return so much actual and perceived value is just one of the reasons why I implore you to take your time with *My Ritual Inventory*, because you've got an incredibly powerful tool in your hands, and there's more to come…

Chapter 13

Using *My Ritual Inventory* as a meaningful ritual

The reason why you added *My Ritual Inventory* to your worksheet is so you can now invoke it daily as a potent meaningful ritual in and of itself. In fact, it was designed specifically to be used as your daily meaningful ritual control center. In it you'll find a convenient and ready source of inspiration whenever and wherever you need one, and a concise guide to all of the people and things that contribute so wondrously to the quality of your life – all on one or two pieces of paper!

In order to invoke *My Ritual Inventory* as meaningful ritual in your life, simply repeat the following two steps for each meaningful ritual on your worksheet:

1. Close your eyes and imagine the ritual for 30-60 seconds. Imagine its unique sights, sounds, aromas, and textures. Imagine how it makes you feel. If it involves other people, imagine their voices, their faces. Meditate for a moment on how it contributes to the enhancement of the assigned basic need(s), and how it improves the quality of your life. In particular, what about it makes you smile and feel loved?

   Your ability to envision each ritual listed on your ritual inventory worksheet is critical to your ability to appreciate it.

2. Say, "Thank you for blessing and enriching my life."

> Remember, gratitude is the primary healing agent, and the reason why so many prayers begin with thanksgiving.

It's that simple. When invoked as a daily ritual, *My Ritual Inventory* becomes a secular prayer of thanksgiving for all of the good people and things that contribute to the quality of your life.

I like to begin each day with *My Ritual Inventory* as a component part of my daily prayer ritual. It imbues me with gratitude and fortifies me for the day ahead. If and when I feel the need for more reinforcement throughout the day or week, I simply take out my worksheet and run through it per the two simple steps above. Each time I do so I rediscover myself, my friends and my passions. *My Ritual Inventory* always works, and I can always adjust it to reflect current exigencies and circumstances in my life.

Likewise, you can always perform *My Ritual Inventory* as a tonic for troubled times. It will always remind you that you are not alone, and that the universe is nothing if not abundant. It will keep you focused on the good people and things in your life, and reduce the amount of time you spend with your own stinking thinking and the stinking thinking of others.

> *One note of caution: Please resist the urge to convert your ritual inventory worksheet into electronic format just so you can invoke it from your smartphone. Doing so will only cheaper the experience each time you use it, and will only reduce its ef-*

fectiveness as an explicit ritual of intervention to help you slow down for a moment or two and offer thanks to all the good people and things that contribute to the quality of your life. The deliberate simplicity and anticipation invoked by removing a precious piece of paper from your pocket and unfolding it in preparation for giving thanks is very much part of the ritual itself, and needs to be respected or it will doubtless become just another mindless thing to rush through en route to something else.

Adding new meaningful rituals to your life

Our lives change. People come and go. Relationships come and go. Sudden and not so sudden changes and disruptions in our lives leave us vulnerable; we find ourselves suddenly back on the outer edge of the human centrifuge, out where we are more likely to choose convenience over quality, out where we are more likely to choose self-serving ritual over meaningful ritual.

Consequently, high stress moments, big lifestyle transitions, and moments of sudden change are especially good times to reassess and adjust your ritual inventory.

Sudden holes in our lives scream to be filled, and all too often we fill them with self-serving rather than meaningful rituals. *My Ritual Inventory* will help ensure that you don't succumb to convenience over quality when the chips are down, when you most need the presence of quality and common sense in your life.

Of course you can invoke *My Ritual Inventory* at any time for any reason, but here's a measured plan to introduce new meaningful rituals over time to help improve the quality of your life, and start moving you closer to the center of the human centrifuge. Remember, however, each new meaningful ritual in your life has the potential to generate big returns per the above examples. So let's proceed slowly, and set realistic goals. Let's start with the introduction of just one new meaningful ritual every other month. One new meaningful ritual every two months may not sound like a lot of progress, but six new meaningful rituals in your life by the end of the first year can yield extraordinary changes.

First, take a few moments to examine the total time you invest in meaningful ritual for each of your four basic needs. Glaring discrepancies in the totals may represent an imbalance in your life wherein some of your basic needs are being satisfied at the possible expense of others. Bear in mind, however, that balance is a relative term, and that how much time you actually invest in meaningful ritual to satisfy each of your four basic needs will doubtless rise and fall as you strive to accommodate changing life circumstances. You may work for months to establish balance in your life across all four basic needs only to experience a sudden seismic event that compels you to reassess and readjust on the fly. For instance, moving to another city to pursue your career may incur long-term benefits across all four basic needs, but the short-term effect will likely be at least physically, emotionally, and socially disruptive – and will likely remain so until you re-establish new relationships and meaningful rituals in your new hometown to restore the balance.

Chapter 13

Next, identify your weakest basic need, defined as the basic need with the lowest perceived time value on your *My Ritual Inventory* worksheet. Over the next week, make it your assignment to identify and incorporate one new meaningful ritual that will enhance and promote your weakest basic need. Finally, add your new meaningful ritual to your *My Ritual Inventory* worksheet and adjust the time totals accordingly; your new meaningful ritual will now assume its place as part of your daily *My Ritual Inventory* review.

Although *My Ritual Inventory* is an incredibly powerful and effective lifestyle improvement tool, it simply cannot help you manufacture more time. So if you're wondering exactly how or where you'll find the time to incorporate another meaningful ritual into your already busy schedule, you need look no further than the *Media Log* worksheet that you created back in Chapter 4. That's where you'll doubtless find the time you need to introduce new meaningful rituals into your life. Remember, it's not about finding more time; it's about replacing self-serving ritual with more meaningful ritual.

> *Repeat the above process once every other month: Identify your weakest basic need, take a week to find and introduce a new meaningful ritual, add it to your worksheet, and adjust the time totals.*

In general, you should look for meaningful rituals that promote moderation over abstinence. And don't overreach; don't set yourself up for failure by expecting yourself to perform miracles, even and especially if you are a classic overachiever. Make modest investments, seek modest gains and let the principle of compounding interest work for you, not only with your money but with your life as well. One year from now you'll enjoy six more meaningful rituals in your life, each contributing disproportionately and aggressively to the overall quality of your life. Moreover, the desire and need to examine and adjust the meaningful rituals in our lives on an ongoing basis is entirely consistent with the fact that the centrifugal force generated by the human centrifuge pushes us inexorably towards life on the edge all the time. *My Ritual Inventory* will help nudge you over time back from the outer edge and closer and closer towards the center. Remember, the quality of your life demands *your* active participation. Do your part and the universe will reciprocate.

We can't stop the human centrifuge from spinning, and we certainly can't stop the centrifugal force winds from blowing. But we can choose quality over life on the edge each and every day. The final chapter of this book will introduce some simple guidelines to help you out…

Chapter 14
Simple rules for a good life...

The following rules are – unlike most rules – not made to be broken, at least not by me. I designed them to improve and protect the quality of my life, and I read through them at least once a day, every day. Feel free, however, to modify them to suit your own sensibilities...

First:
- Begin my day with *My Ritual Inventory*. Doing so compels both humility and gratitude. Humility moderates excess, imposes perspective and promotes patience, and gratitude is the eternal wellspring of all healing.

Next:
- Slow down. Speed kills.
- Encourage then let go of failure in myself and others.
- Deliberately simplify my life at every appropriate opportunity.

Always...
- begin my day with *My Ritual Inventory*.

- try to push communications up the *Emotional Impact Ladder* whenever possible. Pick up the phone or meet in person.
- be a good and true friend. The love I share with my friends is my purest love.
- be respectful and kind to other people and creatures. How they treat me is up to them.
- look to the future with wonderment and open arms. It's coming anyway.
- bring gratitude, passion and patience to every encounter. I'll need them.
- let the people I love know just how much I love them. Life is fragile and uncertain.
- seek wisdom of the ages over knowledge of the moment.
- seek moderation over excess. Excess will always steal my time and freedom.
- seek simplicity over complexity.
- know when to let go.
- love my country, but be skeptical of all technology, all media and all government authority. Skepticism is my first civil obligation in a free society.
- end my day with *My Ritual Inventory*.

Never...
- bring my smartphone to the dinner table.
- check my email when I first wake up in the morning; wait at least one hour.
- use my smartphone in the bedroom as anything except a phone or an alarm clock.
- default to email or text communications when I have the option to phone or meet.

- base my life decisions on fear and envy. Doing so will kill my soul and can only lead to more fear and more envy.
- take my life or the things and people in it for granted. Again, life is fragile and uncertain.
- let anyone tell me what I cannot do. I have the power to change the world.
- surrender my identity or sense of individual right and wrong to any group or institution. Be a good team player but know in my heart that I and I alone am accountable for my life and the decisions I make.
- think of myself as a victim; think of myself as a victor.
- debase my home, family or friends by thinking of or describing them first as financial assets.

Remember...
- that real freedom is the freedom not to participate.
- that I'm not what I eat as much as I am how I eat.
- that for every step I take towards God, God takes two steps towards me.
- that I become my attention.
- that time is my most precious inventory.
- that happiness is a choice I make each and every day.
- that boredom is a reflection on me, not the world around me.
- that all of my choices have consequences.
- that I can't change others. I can only change myself.
- that all healing begins with gratitude and thanksgiving.
- that the people I love want and need to see and hear it from me.
- that I can invoke *My Ritual Inventory* anytime.

Chapter 14

That's all for now. I wish you and yours simple lives of love and grace with good health and peace of mind.

About Jeff Einstein

Jeff Einstein is an entrepreneur, media pioneer, author, lecturer, lifestyle consultant and licensed real estate agent in NYC. His digital chops date back to 1984, when he authored *Einstein's Beginner's Guides*, the first major how-to book series on personal computers, and co-founded Einstein and Sandom Interactive (EASI), the nation's first digital advertising agency. Since then his media work has been featured in virtually every major business print venue, including two front-page articles in *The Wall Street Journal*, and cover stories for *George, Red Herring Magazine, PC Magazine,* and *The New York Times Sunday Magazine*. He has appeared as a media industry expert in dozens of TV and radio interviews, including *CNN 360* with Anderson Cooper, *The Today Show* with Katie Couric and *Lou Dobbs*.

He has nine published titles to his credit, and hundreds of essays and articles. His controversial writings on media and addiction have been published and re-published on literally thousands of websites and weblogs, and he's appeared nationwide as a featured speaker and lecturer at hundreds of trade shows, seminars, and workshops over the past three decades.

Mr. Einstein lives in a quiet suburb of NYC with a wondrous lady and a fierce gato. He tries very hard to be cool for his teenage daughter – who doesn't buy his act for a New York minute.